Ho⋯ RESEARCH

Max M. North, Ph.D.
Pioneer of Virtual Reality Therapy

Richard A. Blade, Ph.D.
Editor-in-Chief,
International Journal of Virtual Reality

Max North

IPI PRESS • COLORADO SPRINGS

Published by **IPI Press**
2608 N. Cascade Ave.
Colorado Springs, CO 80907
Phone/Fax: 1-800-333-0220
International Fax: 719-630-1427
Email: order@ijvr.com

ISBN 1-880930-11-0
Library of Congress Catalog Card Number: 98-91756

Manuscript Editor: Anne German Wilson
Printing and Binding: Morris Publishing

Warning: This publication is designed to provide accurate information in regard to the subject matter covered. However, the authors and publisher assume no responsibility for errors, omissions, or other inaccuracies in the information or material, or from any use or operation of any methods, products, instructions or ideas contained in the material herein.

*We dedicate this book to U. S. Army
Lieutenant Colonel Frank H. Mathis, Jr.
We always remember you!*

1948 - 1998

STUDENT INFORMATION SHEET

This book belongs to: _____

Telephone: _____

E-mail: _____

Course Title: _____

Section: _____

Advisor's Name: _____

Advisor's Telephone: _____

Advisor's E-mail: _____

TABLE OF CONTENTS

SECTION ONE

RESEARCH SKILLS ORIENTATION

INTRODUCTION

Since most people do not read the Preface, I have included the preface for this book at the beginning of the introduction. Very tricky devil am I? Yes, you may have noticed that I am telling you that this book will be very informal and honest. I will use "I" and "we." I also promise, this book, which is well overdue, will give you motivation, courage and insight as well as the technical knowledge and skills you need to conduct meaningful research in the information era and beyond. In the course of reading this book, you may also noticed that the style of writing varies from the usual scientific writing style. It will show you that researchers are people just like you and while they are seriously investigating scientific problems, they can also become careless. Yes, scientists have feelings too. I have been told by my Cyberspace friends that I am "an emotional devil."

Today, many scientific thinkers and scientists are introducing human feelings into their research. I have done this, even though my colleagues and research sponsors think I am on the borderline of reality and fiction. Isn't that where a scientist or artist should be? Should they not be in a position of exploring? I maintain constant communication with other scientists and thinkers and they assure me that I am not alone and that they too have similar points of view. I have to say, by reading this book, we will not only learn and grow together in building skills to do research, but we will have a lot of fun too. This book will show the novice researcher, as well as the advanced researcher, how to build research skills in the current information era from the initial point of having an idea to the point of publishing the research report. Each section will have many examples. Some of the examples are capsulated from the work of my students who represent a cross section of skill levels. Some of the examples are from my own research reports and include a few specific research skill building tasks which ask for information or pose questions for your investigation. At this point, you are expected to secure the approval of your advisor. This approval should be indicated at the bottom of each task box. Your advisor may have devised a different approach for indicating her approval. At any rate, the most important thing is that you complete each task in the time requested. You are also requested to complete the tasks in the order in which they appear in the book. No skipping either! These tasks are designed to assist the researcher in doing a small portion of the research at a time. The basic theory of "divide and conquer," which I will be writing about in a later chapter, is used extensively in my approach. By doing all the tasks in this book, the researcher (I mean you.) will be able to conduct meaningful research and report it in a correct format and style at the end of the semester. Yes, it will be that easy. This is a "how-to-do" book and it is one of a kind. What I am saying, get me to autograph your book before it is too late and do not attempt to sell this book back to the bookstore for a few dollars! I know exactly what students do. I have "been there and have done it all! "

In addition, this book will be written in such a manner that it includes extensive notes from my personal experience as a successful cutting-edge researcher. I know it sounds like I am bragging. This is what other researchers say about my research. I believe we should be proud of our accomplishments and remember that no one else will advertise for us or "toot our horn" but ourselves. Yes, it is time to "wake up and smell the coffee." The old generation of researchers and scientists who waited all their life to be discovered are gone with the dinosaurs. In this information explosion era, it is our responsibility to report our research findings to as many people as we can by using the vast network of professional, scholarly and public media. The other purpose of this book is to serve as a mentor for beginners and to assist advanced researchers.

The content of this book is organized in a unique manner that I learned from previous research students. There are six distinctive sections. Section one is an orientation to research skills, and covers topics such as, Why do research? What is research? types of research, finding a research topic, having an advisor to work with you, ethical issues of research, and emotional factors involved in research.

The virtual library search is discussed in section two. The topics in this section include the reliability of sources, the traditional card catalog, the computerized search, and cyberspace search. Section three is about writing research papers and paying attention to topics such as writing style, research report components, quotations, tables, graphics, illustrations, and ethical issues related to these topics. A generic research approach is described in detail in section four. This section describes the process and assists the researcher in putting together a completed research project. The major components of this section are the title page, abstract, introduction, review of current literature, theoretical framework, methodology, results, conclusions, implications, recommendations, discussion, and references. Section five introduces several topics to assist the researcher in publishing research reports. It discusses how the researcher can select a scholarly publication, submit a manuscript, get it accepted, handle criticism and publish in the popular press. Section six is written by my colleague and co-author of this book, Dr. Richard Blade. He provides insight into the future of information technology. This section is very interesting, inspiring and philosophical.

I suggest that you read the sections, subsections, paragraphs, and sentences in sequential order. If you do not, you will run the risk of getting lost and confused with the jargon, which is designed to help you become familiar with state-of-the-art research information. I do not like the jargon either, but what choice do I have? Not to read? If you choose not to read, you will miss many opportunities to learn; and, believe me, you nor I can afford to miss anything. We already have a lot to catch up on. Don't we?

WHY DO RESEARCH?

No matter who you are, what you do, or where you live, research is effecting your total being. For example, at this moment, scientists are working in the area of Genetic Engineering and running experiments that may alter the essence of the human being. In the very near future, you and I may have several clones who can be in different places at the same time. Advances in aerospace have made it possible to extend our beings to other planets, and very soon we will be able to extend our being to other galaxies and explore the universe. Virtual reality technology can assist you in learning a new behavior to deal with your psychological disorders. It also allows you to recapture the memory of your childhood and explore your mind's universe. This is breakthrough research recently conducted by the lead author, me. Remember, research has produced everything from the clothes you are wearing to the car you are driving, to the processed food you eat. Everyone, including animals, are to some degree involved in the research community. Scientists are continuously, trying to find out about the environment we live in so that we can make intelligent decisions. Simply put, the success of each individual depends on the depth and correctness of the research they conduct.

It is time to do the first task. Remember to do tasks in the order they are presented. I mean it! Be sure to follow my simple instructions.

Task 1 – Give a few more examples of research that you think might radically change your life or the life of others.

So, let me ask you a question. Can you skip research? The honest and intelligent answer is No. Now, it is time to give up and continue to read this book to learn about research technology, its components and see how it is done. As a matter of fact, your research advisor will provide additional motivation to encourage you to read and learn more about research by making completion of this activity a part of your assessment. Your performance will influence the grade you earn. This is a part of your course requirement. I am pleased that now you know I cannot only be informal, but tough too. I strongly advise you to get involved in research. That is the only way you can make sure your opinion counts and to ensure that your discovery and that of others will help our future generations live in peace and harmony with nature and the universe. It will help humanity gain insight into an understanding of the world (Teitelbaum, 1994). So, pay attention to the reference I just made. If you are using someone else's idea, you need to give that person credit. Simply write the name and the year of publication in parentheses and add this information to the reference section of your research report. There will be more about this in later sections.

Task 2 – If you use this book in your research report, how would you reference it?

The most important reason for doing research is to satisfy the requirements of your graduate work. I put this serious matter here intentionally so you will have an understanding of the basic reason for research. As it is said repeatedly, "graduate school is training in research." When you apply for graduate school the first thing the faculty will look for is your skill as a good researcher. You may be surprised to learn that many undergraduate students have already gotten involved in various kinds of research and published their work in scholarly journals and conference proceedings. As a matter of fact, I have advised several of your fellow students to conduct research and write reports. Many of their reports have been reviewed by experts in the field and published in professional journals. A few excerpts from these reports will serve as examples in this book.

It must be noted that, as an undergraduate student, you are expected to do research. The fact that the competition for graduate school is based on active participation in research cannot be ignored. I know the demands of school are getting pretty intense. I realize that you sometimes feel as though you are trapped and have no choice. Yes, it is a fact of life. It is time to begin praying and to light that candle you set aside for special occasions in your religious corner and wish for supernatural powers to do your research for you. Fat chance! The only way to become a successful researcher is to get involved now and keep reading this book. I will be here for you and I know you can do a great job. We may even publish some of your research work too.

Task 3 – List a few more reasons for doing research. I am especially interested in your personal reasons.

WHAT IS RESEARCH?

Please consider asking yourself a simple question, " Which college or university will be better for me to attend?" You may just ask a few friends or relatives about a few schools they have attended to make a decision based on this limited collection of data. You can also go to a library or use the Internet to collect information about colleges and universities. This will help you make a match with the criteria you have constructed for this decision. Based on your research, you may make a different decision or you may narrow your choices. You may talk with some faculty, students and recent graduates from the schools you have chosen. Another option is to check professional journals to find out what kind of research is being conducted at the schools you are considering. Each of these approaches can be helpful; however, the most valid one is to consult the journals. In reality, you can spend the rest of your life trying to determine which university you want to attend. At some point you have to make a decision based on all the relevant factors. This is an ordinary research.

Obviously, the basic difference between a professional researcher and ordinary people is knowing the technology of the research and building skills by repeatedly doing research and gaining experience. For example, when you take your computer for repair, an expert can recognize the problem and with a minimum amount of information, fix the machine. The same task will take you, a novice, longer to complete. (I assume you have no expertise in repairing a computer.)

My major point, contrary to many older researchers, is that all of us who conduct research everyday have the ability to become proficient researchers. Many older researchers will have you believe that their work is complicated and a forbidden area for others. If it is so complicated, how did they learn to do it? Are they aliens from other planets who got training on the planet Zircon? So, do not let them intimidate you with their closed-minds and limited imagination. All of you can learn the technology of research. Remember, I have done it all and have seen it all! So, do not buy any "crab" idea that research is too hard and complicated and that you cannot learn to do it. You would laugh at some of the products professors call research! I told you it would be fun! That is one of the reasons that I am always happy and laughing.

Task 4 – Please give an example of an everyday activity that requires you to do simple research.

Lets look at the nature of research. We all have different internal models of the world of reality or what I like to call perception of reality. There is a real world, which actually exists. How well your perception of reality and actual reality matches shows the degree of your intelligence. We constantly rethink our perception of reality and hopefully we become wiser and closer to actual reality. Let me give you a very simple and childish example. A child does not have a model of the heat from an open fire, until she touches it and learns that it hurts. Once she feels the pain, she has a better model or perception of fire even though this experience does not make her an expert in the field. It adjusted her perception and gave her a better understanding of reality. This is exactly what research is all about. It helps us to understand and closes the gap between what is there and what we perceive to be there. Did it get too philosophical and complicated for you? Tough life! Who said that it would be easy! Not me! Cool off, your advisor will give you a short lecture on this subject.

I will simply say, to do research is a wonderful and exciting opportunity for you to explore the different aspects of a subject area that interests you. It will allow you to increase your knowledge, sharpen your insights, engage your creativity, and possibly make some minute or extensive discovery. The research you will conduct here should make you an authority, if only on a very small portion of a selected subject. This is just the beginning of other opportunities you should take advantage of. I told you that I will direct you on how to build your skills to do research; however, it is up to you to learn what I teach. After this, you should take off on your own. You will feel more comfortable with your research activities and perhaps begin to gain recognition from the research community.

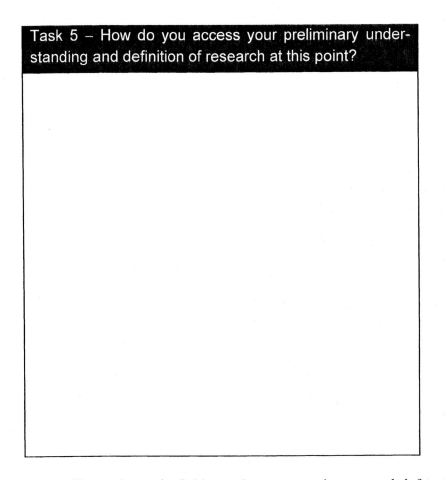

Task 5 – How do you access your preliminary under-standing and definition of research at this point?

The main goal of this section was to give you a brief orientation to research and to combat some of your misconceptions about research. I hope you share with me any information you think I have missed. I would like to include it in the next edition of this book. You can simply contact me by electronic mail (E-mail) at Max@acm.org. See, you are already contributing to the research community.

TYPES OF RESEARCH

Although, there are many types of research, for the sake of simplicity, we can divide research into two general categories, library and experimental. However, it must be noted that the library research is one of the most important components of experimental and any other kind of research. To put it simply, library research is a search of written materials in books, articles in journals, professional conference proceedings, government publications, etc. that are organized as a report. It is really a means of finding out and reporting what is out there. Experimental research is finding out what has been done on a specific area and demonstrating what should be there. In this type of research, the researcher proposes a statement of a problem and hopes to produce a solution for it. Usually, the next step is to set up an experimental design. Once this is done, the researcher determines a methodology (a how-to) for solving the problem. The methodology shows all the steps necessary for possibly solving the proposed problem. This includes defining subjects or participants, the apparatus (e.g., software or hardware needed), the procedures for conducting the experiment, collection of data and statistical analysis of the collected data, if needed. The next step is to report the results of the research. The final step will be to draw conclusions from the results. A discussion step may be added to explain what else can explain the results the researcher has achieved or what else other researchers can do to replicate this research or how is it possible to improve this research. This is only a brief structure of experimental research. More details will be given later.

If you intend to do research in areas such as computer science, engineering, etc., you will find that most of the research conducted by the researchers in these areas are very personalized and in certain cases, it has become their style and signature. The good news is that most of us are pushing for a unified research format, guidelines, and methodology that is consistent with the style and guidelines of what social scientists have established and used for many years. The best example of this notion is our intention to use style and format guidelines from the publication of a manual for the American Psychological Association (APA). To follow the APA style and format will assist us in having a consistent communication packet. Of course, I am pushing this in all aspects of my research. On contrary, it does not limit my imagination and creativity to conduct meaningful and useful research. This matter will be covered in later sections.

I just received an E-mail for Call For Papers (CFP) for an international refereed academic journal. This CFP was encouraging the following kinds of research papers:

- Description of a learning environment
- Theoretical study
- Experimental study
- Literature review
- Methodological study
- Viewpoint

This is the best category of research I have seen yet! Of course, you know by now that I am not claiming to be the authority, but just a humble possessor of knowledge. I will get back to this at the end of the section by getting you to do some task assignments. I also want you to pay attention as new professional jargon is introduced such as CFP, refereed academic journal, etc. By the way, "refereed journal" means that several fellow researchers review a paper that is submitted for publication and may accept the paper with minor modifications, or reject it totally. There will be more about refereed journals in a later section. I know I keep saying that more information will be given in the later sections. Be patient, I need to follow some organization in this book, otherwise I will be lost and confused like you! I will make it my responsibility to introduce to you the professional jargon. I told you that you would be learning and this is just the beginning. By the end of this semester, you will be able to understand what researchers talk about and you can imitate some of their techniques too!

Let me give you another example of how different groups of researchers categorize research or research papers they are soliciting for conferences or journals. This CFP from the Virtual Reality Annual International Symposium '98, sponsored by IEEE, was mailed to my home address. I am a co-chair of this conference. Lucky me! This CFP is for a peer-reviewed (or refereed) conference proceeding accepts either research or applied papers. The CFP describes two categories:

> *"Research Papers should describe results that contribute to the advancement of state-of-the-art virtual reality software, hardware, 3D CHI, or system development."* and

> *"Applied Papers should present a prototype of fielded virtual reality systems. Applied papers should include a concise description of the application area, provide insight into issues relevant to the implementation of the VR system and discuss the effectiveness of the VR system."*

Please note, the technique I used is called a direct code. I used quotation marks to separate them. It is perfectly okay to quote a short paragraph provided you acknowledge the source.

Here is another example of a conference announcement. Unfortunately, I cannot recall the name of the conference. They were soliciting research reports that solve conceptual, methodological, and practical problems. This sounds like three stages of research rather than three types of research! But, who am I to question their authority? As you will see, there are a number of categories and most of them sound right for presenting their perspective.

Now, lets look at how my human-computer interaction/ virtual reality technology group categorizes research. I also refer to this as scientific inquiry. We use this design to conduct our research. We have borrowed it from the social science area. This design is working very well for us and many fellow researchers in computer science, engineering, etc. Please remember that you need to have some models to do research. There are three major categories of scientific inquiry:

(I) Observation – The systematic observation of a phenomenon in its natural state. For example, in human-computer interaction (HCI) research we may simply want to observe the behavior of computer users on a new software or hardware we developed. Our systematic naturalistic observation may give us useful information from which to modify our system in responding more efficiently to the users' needs.

(II) Survey Methods – A more extensive and restricted method of systematic observation. The most popular measurement tools used in this type of research are questionnaires and structured interviews. In addition to observing the users' behaviors, we systematically collect data and utilize the above mentioned measurements. Survey methods are generally used in the study of opinions and attitudes of participants. We usually identify and limit our survey to a particular sample of users. For example, we may study the relationship between the attitudes of freshmen computer users and computer systems we have developed by administering a questionnaire and conducting interviews.

(III) Experimentation – The most powerful extension of observation is experimental research. The researcher not only observes, but manipulates the conditions of the experiment to study the changes in the participants' behavior. For example, in our innovative virtual reality therapy (VRT) research, we defined two groups of participants or subjects. The first group received virtual reality treatment for their psychological disorders and the second group, the control group, did not receive any treatment. This arrangement allowed us to compare the changes in the two groups before and after treatment. We concluded that there was a significant difference between the two groups after the treatment period. It was therefore concluded that the VRT was effective in treating subjects in the experimental group (North et al, 1996).

The following is a brief description of research designs which represent five different categories:

(I) Intensive Case Studies – This design allows for in-depth and comprehensive scientific study. In an extensive systematic case study all the relevant aspects of a phenomenon will be investigated. Usually, we collect a variety of data including the subjective measures or what the users report to us. We also collect the objective measures or the data we collect through our observation or from our instruments. For example, in our VRT research project design, we collected subjective data by asking the participants to report the level of their anxiety in a quantified measurement. We also collected physical objective data from their heart rates every few minutes. Additionally, these two sets of data allowed us to find the relationship between the two measurements. Of course, other forms of data were collected for analysis in our study.

(II) Single Case Experiment – By providing a set of procedures to conduct our intensive case study, we had more experimental control over the variables studied. We call this method the single case experiment. For example, we have developed a virtual reality software to enhance the intrinsic motivation of learners. Thus, to determine the effectiveness of this new software, we devised a detailed step-by-step procedure for the subjects to follow. Basically, we singled out a variable such as software likeability and ran the experiments. At other times, the single case experiment refers to the extensive systematic study of a single subject or participant in an experiment. This approach is great for doing pilot studies and allows us to modify our system or our approach before we begin an extensive experimental research with a large number of participants.

(III) Laboratory Experiments – This kind of experiment allows the investigator to create a simulation of the natural environment for research reasons which may be difficult or impossible to investigate in a real world situation. An example of such a situation is when a researcher uses a laboratory setting or simulated work space to investigate the effect of a newly developed computer software on a group of subjects. The laboratory setting or simulated workspace allows the researcher to have more control over all the variables. In some cases the confidentiality and confidence of the subjects can be preserved better with this kind of research design. Another example is when the research or experiment can be conducted in a weightlessness environment or a space station laboratory to determine which factors cause certain events or changes.

(IV) Traditional Experiments – This is the most frequently used research design in our area. It uses two or more subject groups for experiments. This arrangement permits us to collect measurements from different groups and to make comparisons. An example of our research is the study of virtual reality and performance research we plan to conduct this year. The major goal of this research is to determine the effect of virtual reality on the performance of the simple tasks of picking up objects and placing them compared to the performance of the same tasks in the real world. We will select two groups of subjects for two experiments. One group will interact with objects in the virtual world and the other group will interact with objects in real world. We will ask each group to perform these tasks several times. Measurements of their performance will be collected. The measurements will include the degree of correctness and speed at which the tasks were performed. We will be able to statistically compare the two groups and data from the two experiments to determine if one group is more efficient than the other.

(V) Meta-Analyses – By reviewing the results of independent or similar research studies, you may find different and conflicting results. Believe me, this almost always happens whenever you read the results of research in any field. As a novice researcher, you may feel discouraged and disappointed. However, it is important for you to analyze the research results and determine the average or mean to the results. This method is called meta-analysis (Glass, 1976). For example, Smith and Glass (1977) conducted a meta-analysis of 500 psychotherapy studies and concluded that on average, patients who received treatment did 75% better than patients in the control group who did not receive any treatment.

It must be noted that there are more variations to each of research designs. As you continue to read, you will learn more about these designs. As I mentioned earlier, there are always questions about the validity and reliability of any research method which must concern researchers. This is another reason for you to continue reading and consulting with your research advisor. Our choice of a research design provides guidelines for conducting the research. More information will be given in later sections.

In summary, there are different ways you can categorize research, especially in different discipline. But remember that up to this time, the social sciences seem to have the best documentation for the research types, styles, formats, etc. I have attempted to briefly introduce some of them.

FINDING A RESEARCH TOPIC

Here is the tough time I need to warn you about. This is the time to find a topic for your research or simply figure out what it is that you want to research. So far, my recommendation to my students has been that they must choose a topic they are interested in or that they are curious about. Of course, I am assuming that all of you are novice researchers, otherwise you should not be reading this book. If you know it all, then I suggest that you go about your business and stop criticizing me and my book. What I need to say is, that after you do a few research projects, you will be expected to explore other areas that you might not have much interest in. This will probably be a course requirement. Again, who said that life is fair? So, do not miss the great opportunity you have been granted in this course to do research in your favorite topic! Lucky you! And lucky your advisor!

One shocking fact about research and please do not twist my arms because I cannot recall the source. But I have a hunch that it might be true. Research shows that about 90% of research is either invalid or useless. I almost stopped going to some professional conferences for this reason. It seems that the conferences generate a huge amount of revenue for the organizer(s). They invite a few famous researchers, who need to feed their egos over and over again, and send CFP for other researchers who have been forced by their employers to "publish or parish." Then, there are some others who need to learn how to do research and keep up with the state of that particular discipline, so they register and participate. If you do the mathematical calculation for the income generated by a conference, which may have an average of 2000 participants at a registration cost of $500.00, you will discover that conferences generate a lot of money. As a result, you will see some research papers that have no technical value, yet they get published. I do not want to sound negative, but somebody needs to talk about this problem. Do not get me wrong, there are still gold minds of information at these conference proceedings. There are also excellent professional journals that you can use for your research.

I promised you that I would be honest too! Now you have a pretty good idea of what you have to be careful of. You must be discriminating to select and read any published paper. In general, I limit my students to the primary publications in the computer science area, the ACM (Association for Computing Machinery) and the secondary limited publications by IEEE (Institute for Electronic and Electrical Engineering). However, students are welcome to read lay magazines, newspapers, etc.; but, I do not accept lay publications as references in research reports.

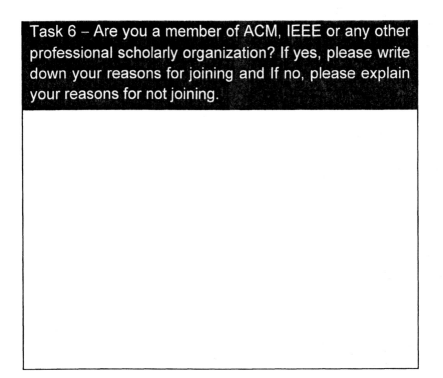

Task 6 – Are you a member of ACM, IEEE or any other professional scholarly organization? If yes, please write down your reasons for joining and If no, please explain your reasons for not joining.

Perhaps this is a good time for you to ask your advisor for the name and contact information for the primary and secondary professional organizations and/or publications in your major. Please note that the ACM has many Special Interest Groups. SIG deals with different areas of computer science. For example, there is SIG for Computer Graphics called SIGGRAPH. I attended a SIGGRAPH conference in 1994 in Orlando, Florida. My attendance was sponsored by a grant from U.S. Army Research

Laboratory (Yes, you need to find sponsors to cover your expenses to the conferences. Believe me, it can be very expensive, even for your teachers). There were over 40,000 SIGGRAPH conference participants from different walks of life from over 32 countries. I heard that since then, the conference has grown to about 80,000 participants.

My major reason for sharing this information with you is to open your eyes to see the different aspects of scholarly meetings. The SIGGRAPH conference, like others, had many components which included technical research reports sessions, demonstration sessions, commercial sessions, discussion sessions, etc. There were scientists researchers, academicians, movie makers, artists, researchers, scientists from all branches of the military, corporations, and most important, there were students. In reality, students were running most of the conferences. Why do students do this? Just to be involved. This is an excellent way to learn about your craft. Most of the students were volunteering their assistance to the conference organizers. This gave them free admission to the conference. Since Atlanta is becoming more attractive to these kind of conferences, you have an opportunity to participate in the major conferences in your discipline and you should do so without any hesitation.

My favorite multidisciplinary SIG is SIGCHI (SIG in Computer-Human Interaction) under the ACM. Not only, I am a member of this SIG, but I am also in the active reviewers' database for their technical research papers. The SIGCHI is your best recourse to collect articles for your research.

SIGCHI is very broad and covers a variety of research activities in their quarterly publication and at the annual conference proceedings. I strongly recommend that all students become members of the ACM and a branch of SIG. That is how you get the latest information you need to survive in your field of study and scholarly work. The fee for students is very minimal. To do so, visit the ACM web site at http://www.acm.org.

Task 7 – Check out the ACM and IEEE web site and write down a summary of what you discover.

There are also other journals that are not affiliated with ACM. They focus on other types of research with specific goals. For example, a new innovative peer-reviewed journal is the International Journal of Virtual Reality, which I contribute to. This is a good source to consult for my area of expertise. The articles are published on a Multimedia CD-ROM using hypertext that includes text, pointers, pictures, sounds, video and movie clips, etc. The other professional journal that I subscribe to is PRESENCE: Teleoperators and Virtual Environments published by MIT (Massachusetts Institute of Technology). I have had the privilege of publishing my research reports and review papers in PRESENCE. The other high quality resources that I either publish in or review papers for are the conference proceedings of the

Human Factors and Ergonomic Society and the Virtual Reality Annual International Symposium sponsored by IEEE. As I mentioned earlier, I am publicity co-chair of the second conference. This is an excellent resource for a researcher. Of course, there are dozen more that I have access to or contribute to in some form. I told you that the secret is to get involved! The quality of the resources the researcher has access to will give her an edge in competing with others.

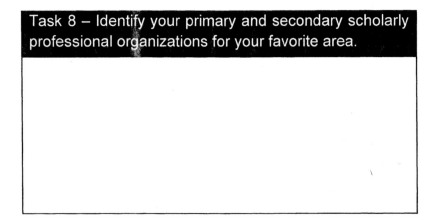

Task 8 – Identify your primary and secondary scholarly professional organizations for your favorite area.

Unfairly, almost all of the research books ignore this section which deals with assisting students in finding a topic. However, as I told you, I will be there for you. This section may become the longest section of the book. I do not care and my editor and publisher are nice and wise enough not to limit me to a certain number of pages or number of words per section.

With the brief background information provided here, it should be easier to understand the process of selecting a researchable topic. The major goal is to choose a research topic that can be used to make a definite contribution to either a body of knowledge or to your own knowledge in your major area.

At this time, I need to inform you that there will be a separate detailed section on the library search. This section will discuss the various methods that can be employed to obtain scholarly publications. That will immediately follow this section. I will give you a brief introduction. You will also be assigned several primary tasks to perform to become familiar with a library search. Sorry, I am trying to give some organization to this book while providing you with information you need at the right place and the right time.

The first and most important recommendation is that you choose a topic you are interested in or that you have some curiosity about a topic to investigate. If you like or love what you do, generally, you will do a better job! I know I told you this before, but it does not hurt to repeat! The second recommendation is that you either go to a library or use your virtual library through the Internet connection on the computer. The latter is called Cyberspace.

Task 9 – Find the Internet address for three virtual libraries.

Most libraries are on-line and will assist you in finding any article you are looking for. This is like looking for a gold mine! Whether you are using the physical library or virtual library, you will have access to a computer to do your preliminary search. There will be more about this later. You will have to enter a few key words that describe your topic to begin the search. For example, you may enter "Virtual Reality" as key words for your search. Fortunately, there is a tremendous amount of information in Cyberspace and you will get thousands of hits or pointers to web sites which contain the words Virtual Reality.

Task 10 – Begin your search. How many hits did yet get when you used the keyword "Virtual Reality? List the number of abstracts available in the physical (regular) library or the virtual library.

Now you need to narrow your search. The quickest way is to limit the search to the last five years of publication. This move will provide you with recent articles and hopefully the most current information in the filed. However, in any field there are classic publications that were published earlier and you cannot ignore them. How do you recognize the classic articles? You look at the reference section of the newer articles. The classic articles will be listed as references if they reported important research in the field. This does not mean that the older publications will not contain information that will be relevant to your research. Sometimes the classic articles are like finding gold and give researchers a direction or point of view to look at the current problem.

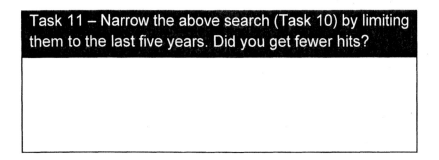

Task 11 – Narrow the above search (Task 10) by limiting them to the last five years. Did you get fewer hits?

The next step in narrowing your search is to read a few article headings or look up a few on web sites. Did I say the forbidden word, *READING*? Sorry folks, who said that life is fair? So far there are two major things you have to do to become good at research, one is to get *Involved*, two is to *Read*. I know the new generation hates to read, but I have not found another alternative yet. When I find it, you will be the first to know. Therefore you need to *read*, *read*, and *read*.

Task 12 – Narrow your search by using additional key words, if possible. What was the outcome?

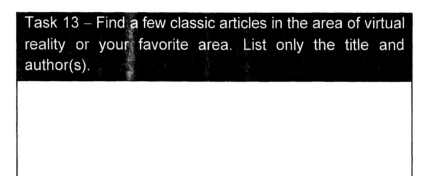

Task 13 – Find a few classic articles in the area of virtual reality or your favorite area. List only the title and author(s).

When I read the headings of articles, I view them as a crude summary. You will also encounter more key words in the headings. These are the secondary key words that you can pick up and reenter in your search window to narrow the topic. You may still get hundreds of hits or if you are lucky you may get just a few. I usually continue the process until I get a manageable number of articles. For me, about 10 to 20 articles will do. At this point, you start reading more and more. You not only read the titles of the articles, you read the abstracts as well. I look at the abstracts as a more extensive summary of the article. And believe me, there are many more key words there that may help you narrow your search, if needed.

Another secret of our trade is that, most of us just read the abstracts of most articles. This is the only way we can stay up-to-date with the tremendous number of publications in an area. So reading abstracts is one of the major tasks of the researcher. Begin to read! At this point, you should have narrowed your search to a few articles.

Task 14 – At the end of your search, get a print-out of those selected abstracts and list at least five titles here.

Now, get copies of the articles, find a quiet place, a high-lighter and begin to read. Even, if you find only one interesting article in this manner, I congratulate you and call you a winner. If you did find an article you can use, I recommend that you repeat the process until you find the "golden egg."

Task 15 – Read the abstracts and present them in your class. Use only five minutes for the presentation of each article. Write the titles of three of the abstracts here.

One more recommendation is that you check the list of references for each article. You will find additional references that you can look up. I have discovered an average of ten to thirty references in most papers. This multiplies your opportunity to find just the right article(s) for your research. What a great opportunity! Lucky you!

When I am reading an article, I try to understand what the researcher is reporting. I make notes on how I can expand the research or give it a new dimension. This becomes a part of my agenda for new research.

Task 16 – Write down how you can improve or extend one of the articles you selected.

The other way I locate a research topic is to completely read all the articles I have selected before selecting a favorite. Then, if I do not like something about the way the research was done, the least I can do is to replicate it. It should definitely be done with definite and clear reference being made to the original article.

Task 17 – Find your favorite article and describe how you would like to replicate the research in a new fashion. Would you make any modifications?

Many good research articles include a section on future research. Actually this is an important part of the criteria for me when reviewing papers for journals as either a reviewer or editor. A good research report should direct the readers to future research needed or unanswered research questions that others can follow. You must agree with me that this is a tremendous help for novice researchers.

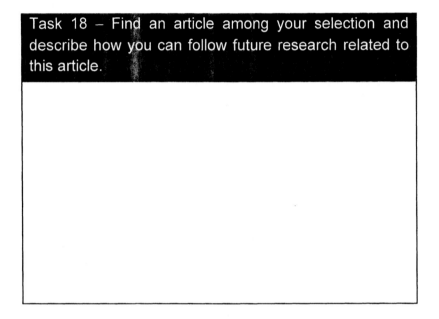

Task 18 – Find an article among your selection and describe how you can follow future research related to this article.

Of course, as you improve your research skills, and believe me you will, you will discover your own "niche" and territory to explore. And quite possibly, you will have your name listed in future scholarly journals, books and other publications.

The other techniques I have used that work well with students is to ask each student to read, summarize, and make a presentation of her selected article or articles. During or at the end of the presentation, I introduce different ideas that students can use as topics for research. Sometimes, other students offer their thoughts and ideas. This creates a good discussion session, food for thought and new research ideas to pursue.

Task 19 – Participate in the class discussion when students report and give a summary of articles, then list a few research ideas introduced to the class by your advisor.

Task 20 – Now, list a few research ideas introduced by you and your classmates in the discussion session.

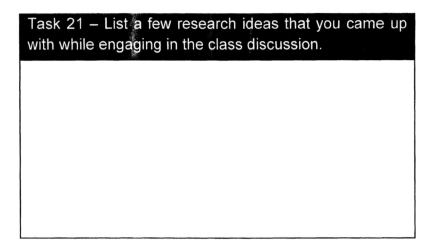

Task 21 – List a few research ideas that you came up with while engaging in the class discussion.

Since I have been in this business of research for many years, I have developed close contact with many other researchers in my field. We consult by e-mail or telephone. I have made it my job to know the top 20% of the researchers in my area and related areas. I met many of these people at conferences or through Cyberspace communication. If I need any reference, or even brain storming, I send an E-mail to my mailing list and ask for their help. There are also several students on my mailing list too. I get a tremendous amount of help from them as well as from the better known researchers. You need to be involved and know at least five top researchers in your field. You should also make it a point to read their research reports and contact them personally. I did tell you that they are just like you, human. In most cases, they get excited to know somebody out there is interested in their work. In some cases they may even provide you with the research reports that they have not published yet. This is a fantastic opportunity because, journal articles may take up to two or even three years to appear. I understand that, that is very long time, but the queues are backed up. Additionally, there are several levels in the review process. Therefore, I suggest that you get all the help you can. There are also professional discussion lists that you can join. These discussion lists generate a lot of new ideas, point of view, thoughts etc. that you can use for your research topic.

Task 22 – Find out the top 10 percent of the researchers/ scientists in your area of study and list their names and some of their publications. Two to five names will be enough.

Task 23 – Search for their E-mail address or their Web sites using the Internet search engines. (e.g., Yahoo™).

Task 24 – Go ahead and send them an E-mail. Tell them you are a student looking for their latest or current research publications etc. Ask questions about research. Write down your action(s).

Task 25 – Now list the latest research articles of the researchers you could contact, including the author(s)' name, year of publication, title of the article, name of the publication, and page numbers.

One of the major problems that seems to hound student researchers is that they select a broad topic for their first research project and attempt to do a grandiose work. They try to solve all the problems of the universe with a one-semester research project. They need to divide the topic into subtopics. And, if that is too much to deal with, divide it further and further. You are expected to do research about a very narrow topic and make a small contribution at this time. It is really a skill to be able to narrow the scope of the research topic. This is another good reason to have your advisor around. At this time our motto goes like this: *Get Involved, Read,* and *Communicate.*

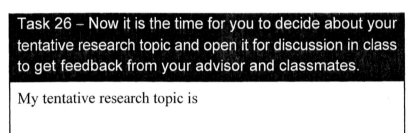

Task 26 – Now it is the time for you to decide about your tentative research topic and open it for discussion in class to get feedback from your advisor and classmates.

My tentative research topic is

This section is long; so, I do not mind apologizing. I am human like you. Surely, there are unlimited ways to find topics. I just gave you a few techniques to use. Actually, I am looking forward to collecting more ideas for the next edition of this book from students as well as the faculty. The bad news is that this section would be much longer since it is the heart of the research process. The good news is that your advisor(s) and I are here to help you. At this stage you simply need to determine what topic you will research. And, as my students say, "There are too many to choose from! "

> Task 27 – Please, write down your ideas on how to find a research topic. Does it differ from what I have already discussed in this book? Please E-mail a copy of your ideas to me at Max@acm.org.

YOUR ADVISOR(S)

Now that you have your tentative topic, you need to select an advisor to work with you. You might be limited to your current professor. Most professors are willing to hear from you. Don't be too shy to ask for help. Actually, discussing your research topic and ideas for your research not only excites you, but your advisor and other faculty as well. Communication is the key at this point.

Please take this advice to heart and do not limit your communication to your major advisor. Use any researcher, scientist, professor or student who is doing research. Your research will be made better by the additional points of view you get. These people also have their own resources that they might be willing to share with you.

To have an effective communication with your advisors, you need to learn their language as well. There is nothing better than spending time with them and getting to know them. As I told you before, advisors like researchers are human too and have a need to socialize and communicate with others. Here are some tips E-mailed to me by a friend. What professors say and what they really mean... When they say "Not much is known about..." they really saying that "I don't know anything about..." or when they say "Well, that answer would be beyond the scope of this course." they wanted to say that "I haven't a clue." You might take these examples as jokes as they were intended to be, but there is some merit to it that advisors/professors have their own language too!

Task 28 – Communicate with a few of faculty to find out about the research they are conducting. List their research.

Specially, if you are doing your thesis or dissertation, you have the opportunity to have more than one advisor to assist you in doing your research. Usually not less than three advisors and does not mean that you cannot have more experts to help you.

Make friends with your advisors, that includes inviting them to lunch, and hope they will discuss the research they are conducting. If so, it will be to your advantage to volunteer to work with them. This collaboration is very fruitful for both of you. The advisor gets some help and you get a "fast food" version of a possible research topic. You can get permission to simply work on the research currently in progress. Although this is the way it happens in most graduate schools, it may not be possible to duplicate the same model with 1500 or more freshmen in our university. Frankly, it may not be impossible. Of course, I have removed the word "impossible" from my personal vocabulary. What I am trying to say to you is that any thing is possible providing to find out how to do it. This was just a brief lesson for you to think positively and optimistically about your favorite topic of research and do not limit yourself at all.

If you, an undergraduate, are lucky enough to find a research advisor, I am happy for you and wish you the best. But, since 99% of you will not have such a privilege, you need to depend on yourself, read and follow the instructions in the previous sections which show you how to find a topic. As I mentioned earlier, the Human-Computer Interaction Group will be available to you to discuss your ideas and topics at any time. This does not mean that other faculty of the Computer and Information Science Department and other departments are not willing to work with you. You need to ask, and hopefully you will receive the help you are looking for.

Task 29 – Now it is time for you to select an advisor to assist you in your research. List his/her name, research area, and a few of the recent publication.

ETHICAL ISSUES OF RESEARCH

You may wonder why I am including ethical issues of research in this section rather than in the Appendix. My reason for doing is that I want to make sure you read this now and not postpone your reading or, God forbid, ignore reading at all. Many of my fellow researchers and I believed students did most of the cheating that occurred in research. An article that appeared in the ACM last year shocked me. The article showed that the faculty researchers admitted to cheating on their research with much more frequency than their students. So I stopped blaming my students and began to read more about the code of conduct in the research. Please pay attention to what I am going to say. If you cheat on your research, how will you ever know whether your ideas and your research work or not? What about all the time and energy you put in to cover up a big lie and other questions that will come up?

Any senior researcher will tell you that it takes more time and energy to cheat than it takes to be honest and really conduct the research. Please accept what we say and save yourself and your reputation. Most of us know when you have illegally copied someone else's work or fudged your data, even though we may not confront you every time. Based on the ACM article, we professionals have more experience in cheating than you! Note that I did not give you the exact information about this article, because I could not find the journal on my bookshelf. I think one of my students borrowed it without my permission. Please do not use any information that you cannot provide reference for. I can get by, since my words have more authority than yours. You should not do this!

I am not sure that there is anybody other than yourself to convince you that cheating in research is time consuming and sometimes embarrassing. Of course there are many more side effects which are not within the scope of this book. Perhaps that would be in my next book. The easiest way to do research and feel good about yourself is to follow the professional code of ethics. I will list the code for you in the following section.

As you may have figured out by now, the professional code of ethics must have been addressed and documented by many research organizations. For example, ACM, IEEE, and APA have developed their version of the professional code of ethics, which deals with such issues as perceptions of fairness for research. I advise you to obtain and read the article, *Is my research ethical?* by George T. Duncan published in the Communication of the

ACM (Duncan, 1996). This article specifically discusses the criteria for ethical research on the Internet.

The guidelines for conducting research, which I prefer, is a very comprehensive but effective set of guidelines written by Dr. Justin Zobel in the Department of Computer Science, RMIT, Melbourne, Australia. With his permission for reprint in this book, here is a summary of his March 1997 paper, "Guidelines for the Conduct of Research." It must be noted that because the article is relevant to this section of the book, I have included it here. I am including the summary portion at this point. Other parts of the Code will be listed at the appropriate section of this book.

One might ask why I have selected a paper from an Australian author and not one from someone in the United States. Research is a global activity. We can no longer ignore the rest of the world and put our heads in our shell and refuse to see the research works from other countries. Some of these international works are of a very high quality. In my opinion and the opinion of other researchers, we need to be open-minded and learn that we are not the only country with great scientists and researchers. As a matter of fact Dr. Zobel is an active member of ACM SIGMOD and has published similar papers in this country. Here is the unedited text of the report:

The broad principles that guide research have been long established. Central to these are the maintenance of high ethical standards, and validity and accuracy in the collection and reporting of data. [Australian Vice-Chancellors' Committee' s Guidelines for Responsible Practice in Research (AVCC)]

The process of research—that is, the discovery of scientific truths—relies on the assumption that researchers observe ethical guidelines, but these guidelines are often unstated or implicit. These guidelines concern the conduct of research, including ethical considerations, retention of data, content of published material, plagiarism, authorship, and refereeing. The principle recommendations are that:

- Research workers are committed to high standards of professional conduct.

- Research workers should only participate in work which conforms to accepted ethical standards and which they are competent to perform.

- Confidentiality must be observed.

- Data—the outcomes and results of research—must be recorded in a durable and appropriately referenced form.

- The minimum requirement for authorship of a publication is participation in conceiving, executing or interpreting a significant part of the outcomes of the research reported.

- Supervisors should ensure that the work submitted by research students in the work of the student.

- Supervisors must not publish a student's work without giving appropriate credit (usually authorship) to the student.

- Researchers should not referee a paper or examine a thesis where there is a real or perceived conflict of interest, or where there is some reasonable likelihood that it will be difficult for the referee to maintain objectivity.

The recommendations are based on several sources, principally the AVCC guidelines quoted above. This document is advisory only and does not have the status of regulation. Three of the AVCC's general ethical considerations are of particular relevance to Computer Science:

- It is a basic assumption of institutions conducting research that their staff members are committed to high standards of professional conduct. Research workers have a duty to ensure that their work enhances the good name of the institution and the profession to which they belong.

- Research workers should only participate in work which conforms to accepted ethical standards and which they are competent to perform. When in doubt they should seek assistance with their research from their colleagues or peers. Debate on, and criticism of, research work are essential parts of the research process.

- If data of a confidential nature is obtained ... confidentiality must be observed ... In general, however, research results and methods should be open to scrutiny by colleagues within the institution and, through appropriate publication, by the profession at large.

In this context, data does not necessarily include the subject of an experiment—by analogy, a chemist is not required to keep test-tubes of chemicals once the work is complete—but rather the outcomes, results, and conclusions of research.

Researchers are trusted to observe good conduct, which is based on the following guiding principles:

- Research is the pursuit of truth,
- Researchers should, in all aspects of their research,
    - demonstrate integrity and professionalism,
    - observe fairness and equity,
    - avoid real or apparent conflicts of interest;

- Research methods and results should usually be open to scrutiny and debate by other researchers and, through publication, by their profession.

Misconduct in research includes:

- Fabrication of data and claiming results where none have been obtained;
- Falsification of data including changing of records;
- Plagiarism, including the direct copying of textual material, the use of other people's data without acknowledgement, and the use of ideas from other people without adequate attribution;
- Misleading ascription of authorship including the listing of authors without their permission, attributing work to others who have not in fact contributed to the research, and the lack of appropriate acknowledgement of work primarily produced by a research student or assistant;
- Any practice that seriously deviates from those commonly accepted within the research community;
- Intentional infringement of published Codes of Conduct.

Misconduct does not include honest errors or honest differences in interpretation or judgements of data; but significant errors should be corrected as promptly as possible.

Accusations of misconduct or unethical behavior are serious matters and should only be made after careful consideration. Adequate protection of the complainant and the accused demand absolute confidentiality.

Task 30 – Summarize these code of ethics and discuss them in the class. Five minutes should be sufficient.

Task 31 – Now it is time for you to think of what other code of ethics might be missing from the guidelines presented here and list them.

EMOTIONAL FACTORS OF RESEARCH

Although this title is placed here to give you a brief account of the emotional factors involved in research, I should say that emotional factors like the ethical issues are involved in every step of research activities. (I will be reminding you where ever it occurs.) For the sake of simplicity, I will discuss some of these issues at this point.

First of all, research is not an easy task. Even though I am trying to break down the components of research and make it simple. Research requires time, persistence and patience. There are more ABD (a doctoral students who has done All But Dissertation is called ABD—not an official title) in graduate programs than there are undergraduates. The main reason they have not been able to complete their dissertations is they become frustrated with their research activities. Some try for years and constantly fail and take the failure personally. It is not uncommon for people in this category to be faced with psychological issues. They forget research involves taking risks. On the other hand, it is important to remember that you are doing something new and no one knows if the project fails or succeed. Just take a chance!

On a personal note, many of my projects have failed several times before they worked properly. I keep track of all of my failures and hope I do not repeat the failures. Some of the procedures and even software that did not work properly in some of my projects proved to be fully functional and successful for other projects. I believe failures are the building blocks of success. I know it does not feel good to deal with failure, but it is a necessary step in the process. This might have become obvious to you, but I felt it was important to mentioned it.

You need to make research a part of your daily routine. You will be surprised to find that many researchers get up in the middle of night and jot down notes and come up with the solution to a problem they have been working on. This can happen after days, weeks, or months of waiting for a fresh new idea. Therefore, my advice to you is to not give up and to keep the research problem in mind at all times. Anticipate that breakthrough you have been waiting for. Research always takes more time that you or your advisor can predict. If you are a novice researcher, every step takes more time. Be kind to yourself!

When I complete any research project, I feel relief and relaxed for a short while; however, there is always a feeling that my project is not worthwhile. Of course, as soon as I receive the first E-mail, telephone calls, and regular mail from the other scientists, researchers and even the popular media, I begin to feel that I contributed to the body of human knowledge. For the novice researcher, this feeling of self-doubt is much worst. I must remind you that, at this point, you should have made many right decisions (based on your informal research) in your life because you are reading this book. And remember that doing good research takes skill and needs conscious and active involvement. That simply means that you deserve to be here and your ideas are worthwhile. We will help you to conduct worthwhile research and report it too. This somehow should take care of a portion of your negative feelings!

Data taken from a survey of a group of about fifty Noble Peace Prize winners in science reported the feelings of the scientists in regard to self-doubt about their work. They were unanimous in their response regarding their perception of personal doubt about the value, or correctness, of their work. They all experienced periods when they felt that what they were doing was irrelevant, obvious, or even wrong. This is not a bad thing, as scientists and researchers, having doubts about our own research is a good sign. Being a critical evaluator of one's own work and, sometimes others, ensures quality. We should not allow negative feelings to stop us from conducting research.

If you are one of those people who cannot work alone, please find a collaborator. The good part of having others work with you is that you can always blame them for your failures. I am just kidding! That would not be fair. For example, if you look at research articles published by the APA, you will be surprised to find that most of the articles have more than two authors or collaborators. I have seen as many as ten authors. Mostly M.Ds. (Medical Doctors). If they can work together with their hectic professional life, why we should be working alone? Collaborative work will also help you develop the skills you need for team working situations. It allows you to hear feedback or give suggestions to fellow researchers. There is much to be said about the advantages of collaboration. Simply take my word and do it!

Task 32 – List additional emotional factors that you might have discovered in the class discussion session.

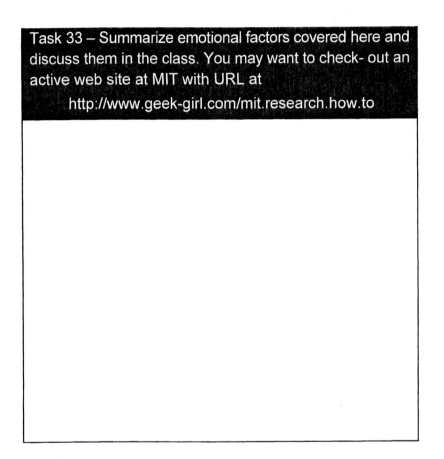

Task 33 – Summarize emotional factors covered here and discuss them in the class. You may want to check- out an active web site at MIT with URL at
http://www.geek-girl.com/mit.research.how.to

At this time, I hope you have a good idea and feeling about research and that you are ready to passionately go forward. And again, I promise you, we are all there to assist you. This is the main reason I spent my summer break writing this book.

The technical materials will be coming in the next four sections. They will be presented in a more intense fashion. Therefore, I recommend that you read this chapter as many times it takes. Do all the tasks assignments at the end of this section before you proceed. Good Luck!

Task 34 – Please list briefly how your perception of research has changed so far from reading this book. Also state why and how you might get more involved in research.

REFERENCES

Duncan, T.D. (1996). Is my research ethical?,*Communication of the ACM 39*,12, pp. 67-68.

Glass, G.J. (1976). Primary, secondary and meta-analyses of research. *The Educational Researcher, 5*, pp. 3-8.

North, M.M., North, S.M., & Coble, J.R. (1996). *Virtual Reality Therapy: An innovative paradigm*. Colorado Springs: IPI Press.

Smith, M.L., & Glass, G.J. (1977). Meta-analyses of psychotherapy outcome studies. *American Psychologist, 32*, pp. 752-760.

Teitelbaum, H. (1994). *How to write a thesis, a guide to the research paper*. New York: Arco Publishing, Prentice-Hall.

Zobel, J. (1997). Guidelines for the conduct of research. *Department of Computer Science, RMIT,* Melbourne, Australia.

SECTION TWO

THE VIRTUAL LIBRARY

One of the major components of any research project is library resources. "Your research is as good as your library resources. You are what you read." Fortunately, today you have access to, what I call, the virtual library through Electronic Databases and the World Wide Web (WWW). Lucky you! What a great time to conduct research! Obviously,because of the databases and Internet, the way library searches are done has changed; therefore, we need to learn new strategies to deal with inquires.

This section concentrates primarily on the virtual library and starts with a brief introduction to computerized databases that contain bibliographic references and Internet resources. However, if you are following my recommendation of reading this book and doing the tasks in a sequential order, you have already encountered the section which discusses finding your favorite topic. I will repeat some of the strategies here. Repetition does not hurt! I will give you a few clues on how to execute a search on databases; you must learn the specific commands for each search engine. Sorry! It is impossible to include over 250 databases in this book! Regardless of which resources you intend to use, the primary goal is to locate relevant literature for your research. Since we are planning to conduct scholarly research, we have to limit our references to books, scholarly journals, articles, professional conference proceedings, graduate theses and dissertations, etc. Some references were mentioned in section one. At this point, you should know authors' articles or which publications you need.

RELIABILITY OF SOURCE

The reliability of resources, especially materials on the Internet, has become more fragile. Almost anyone or any group can set up a web site on the Internet. There is no check or evaluation of what goes on the Internet. Although it is the most democratic method for presenting personal or group materials and points of view, it poses issues of reliability. Simply because something is posted on the Internet does not mean it is valid or reliable. It is your responsibility to verify materials you plan to use as references for your research.

I will give you a few personal recommendations for evaluating resources. The first thing I check is the name of the author or authors. As I mentioned earlier, you need to know the top researchers in your area. This will help you verify the validity of the materials you choose to use. The next thing I do is check out the organization or the research group the author(s) are affiliated with. For instance, If the organization is a well-established university or department of the university involved in my area, that is a good indication of the reliability or trustworthiness of the source. The next thing I check is the publisher of the research. Publishers usually evaluate their authors' work and, to protect their investment, do not invest in the less known authors. There are always exceptions to the rule. Sometimes their decision is based on sales rather than the quality of the material. Remember, you are the judge; and, reading the material is the most effective way to evaluate it.

Again, no matter what technique you use for evaluation, gradually your experience and intuition will guide you through the process. I recommend that, for this current course, you stay with publications from ACM, IEEE and a few others I introduced in section one and you will be fine. I told you I would make it easy for you. Lucky you!

Task 35 – Write down the list of tentative topic(s) you plan to focus on and conduct research on.

Task 36 – Have you decided which library resource you will use for your research? If so, please list them.

THE TRADITIONAL CARD CATALOG

The card Catalog is an index of the library holdings. It appears to be the most inconvenient tool for conducting a search in any library. Frequently, it is hard to find information that you know is in the library. In some libraries you have no other choice but to learn the system and use it.

Task 37 – Go to your institution's library and look at the card catalog used there. What do you think of it?

Fortunately, most college and university libraries have a computerized database of their holdings. They also have access to databases of the materials not physically available at their library. Regardless of the classification method used by the library, holdings are indexed alphabetically by author's last name, title, and subject. The bad news is that the primitive card catalog does not list the individual articles, essays, etc. in each book, especially in periodicals. You should consult with your librarian to find out which general indexes you need to use to do your research. This is a good time to make another friend, the librarian! It does not hurt to send him or her a thank you note from time to time. Remember, they are there to help you and they have the skills you need. Believe me, you can save a lot of time by just asking first. You may not believe me if I tell you that I rarely looked in the card catalog for my research, even during the earlier stage of my career.

Task 38 – Are you having any problems locating a particular article? If so, what are the problems?

Task 39 – Did you meet your personal librarian? List his or her name, telephone number and job title here.

THE COMPUTERIZED SEARCH

Did I "nag" you about the card catalog and push you to use the computerized search to find your favorite materials? As I mentioned earlier, there are many databases with their own search engines. Each of the databases is specialized or limited to a specific area. For example, PsycLIT™ and PsycINFO™ databases provide you psychological abstracts. A few other popular databases are InfoTrac™, ProQuest™, ERIC™, Medline™. I covered the general strategy to use to execute a search on any of the databases. Basically, you have to work with keywords or search terms to locate your favorite paper(s). The keyword is what you think should describe the paper(s) you are looking for. Most journals and conference proceedings have a section in each article in which the author(s) is asked to provide the keywords related to the content of the paper. For example, most of my papers in the virtual reality area have several keywords such as, *virtual reality, virtual reality therapy, virtual environments*, etc. Remember, these keywords are sometimes the jargon the researchers or scientists use in their research reports. They do vary; however, when these keywords are consistently used by more of my fellow researchers, they make their position more prominent. For example, the word, *database,* now is an accepted jargon and keyword to locate literature.

Task 40 – What computerized databases does your library use? List their names here.

Task 41 – Locate the articles you need for your research and use proper key words. How many articles did you find?

In reality, your major job, at this point, is to find several good keywords for your search task. It is not an easy task! Again, the more you read scholarly papers, the more you will know about the keywords. In general, most of the search engines or software allows you to use Boolean connectors such as *and* and *or* for use with your keywords. The word *and* used between the keywords will locate all the abstracts which contain all the keywords you provided. And by using the word *or* between the keywords, the search will list any abstracts which contain either or all of the keywords. It is very logical! All libraries will provide you with a brief instruction template for building more complicated search queries.

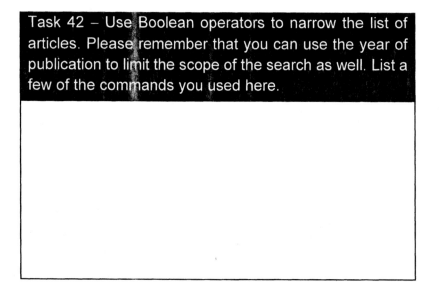

Task 42 – Use Boolean operators to narrow the list of articles. Please remember that you can use the year of publication to limit the scope of the search as well. List a few of the commands you used here.

The most important thing is that you find the right database and right keywords to use in searching for the article(s) in the area you are interested in. Like anything else, it takes time and skill, which you will gain by just practicing.

As I mentioned in section one, there are two situations you may encounter while conducting a computerized search. The first is that you may get more abstracts than you care to read. The number can be as many as a few hundred or even a thousand. Regardless of the kind of search you use, the general strategy is to narrow the list by typing in more keywords. You need to continue this process until you get as many articles or abstracts as you can manage to read. I usually keep about twenty-five abstracts. I read and grade them by putting three stars on the best matches, two stars for a good matches and one star for the "okay" ones. The next thing I do is to get the full article for as many of the three-star rated abstracts as I can. In some cases, the abstract is all you can get. Do not ask me why, since I have posed this question to several librarians. The most common reply was that they were not able to locate the entire paper at that time. My next step is always to try to find articles for the two-star rated abstracts. This process is continued until I get as many of the selected articles as possible. The other useful technique is to get one of the articles from the top of your priority stack and look in the reference section. The reference section of the article will provide additional related articles to search for.

The second situation is that you do not get any "hit" from the key words, you need to expand your search by either dropping keyword(s) or reorganizing them. In some search engines I have had to start from the beginning and use alternative keyword(s). And, to my surprise, I got a different list of abstracts. This is the nature of most search engines. The point is, do not give up easily and say, " I cannot find anything." Of course, there may be times when you will be researching an area of research for which there is limited reference information. When this is the case, I tell my students that they are very lucky! Because they have identified an area that is either new or very narrow; therefore, they have a great opportunity to explore the new possibilities. The final point is, that either way, it is good news!

Task 43 – Now after ranking your articles' abstracts, try to find the entire article or articles from the abstracts. I suggest, at this time, that you ask the librarian for help. Write about this experience.

Task 44 – Which method is easier for you–the card catalog or computerized databases?

CYBERSPACE SEARCH

Immediately you may ask me, "What is Cyberspace?" Different people describe it differently. That was too obvious! I told you I am smart! "Cyberspace, the new frontier" by William Gibson is described as:

> "A consensual hallucination experienced daily by billions of legitimate operators, in every nation, by children being taught mathematical concepts... A graphical representation of data abstracted from banks of every computer in the human system. It is an unthinkable complexity, lines of light arranged in the non-space of the mind, clusters and constellations of data. Like city lights, receding..."

My simple definition for cyberspace is that it is the space where the collective universes of the mind meets. Whatever the definition is, it does not matter. What matters most is that there is a tremendous amount of literature floating in cyberspace and one needs to learn to access it effectively. The most simple approach to use one of the existing search engines on the Internet, such as Excite™. Enter the keywords, *Virtual Library*. I did and got a lot of hits. Here are a few of the top ten matches:

The World-Wide Web Virtual Libraries:
　　　　http://www.ikts.ghg.de/veramics.html
　　　　http://cdr.stanford.edu/html/WWW-ME/home.html
　　　　http://www.comlab.ox.ac.uk/archive/other/museums.html
　　　　http://physiology.med.cornell.edu/WWWVL/PhysioWeb.html
　　　　http://www.dataspace.com:84/vlib/comp-graphics.html
　　　　http://www.lib.lsu.edu/databases/

Task 45 – Find a few more definitions for Cyberspace from the Cyberspace search and list them here.

Task 46 – Locate a few more virtual libraries from Cyberspace and list them below.

As you can see, cyberspace is a new frontier for exploration. The main idea of this section was to briefly introduce you to pointers you need in order to locate your favorite research articles. And do not forget your main resource site, the ACM, which has abstracts of the articles they publish. The articles can be accessed through the ACM web site. This source may be sufficient for you in the beginning. Later you will be expected to locate other sources as well.

Task 47 – Go back to the ACM web site and locate the articles you may need for your research. List the titles.
The URL address for ACM is http://www.acm.org

I know I am cutting this section short. Believe me, you must try it yourself. If you do not, it makes no sense for me to write and for you to read about it. This is the time when you need to "roll up your sleeves" and "get to it".

Each person will gain a different insight and new skills by going after the information they need. Basically, all you have to do is to get access to the Internet and use one of the existing search engines, such as Yahoo™, Excite™, Lycos™, etc. Do not forget to use the proper keywords to locate what you need. You may want to read the first section of this book again and take more notes. There will be several hands-on sessions with your advisor for this course at this time. Then you are on your own! Good Luck!

Task 48 – Did you find all of the articles you needed? If so, list the titles of the articles you will definitely use in your research. If no, you need to get help from your advisor.

Task 49 – Please list any other strategies you used to locate the articles other than the ones listed in this section. List them in order of importance. I encourage you to send a copy of this to my E-mail (Max@acm.org).

Task 50 – Now that you have the articles in your posses-sion, please let others know how you got them. With the permission of your advisor, share your experience with your class during a discussion period. Write a summary of the class discussion.

WRITING THE RESEARCH PAPER

This section will provide a brief description of issues that deal with writing your paper. However, you may say that you are not ready to write your research paper yet. I know that you are still reading the articles you collected. At least that is what you promised to do. And believe me, if you are not reading those wonderful articles, you are wasting my time and yours.

Please be reminded that this section is just an introduction and will be very brief. For a comprehensive coverage of writing techniques and styles, you need to consult technical books. Here are some resources you may need to consult for your research:

- A good dictionary like Webster.
- Roget's Thesaurus and a good writer's handbook on grammar and usage.
- Harbrace's College Handbook, a writing guide.
- Masters theses index, a Guide to Bibliographies of Theses, U.S. and Canada.

- Guide to Doctoral Dissertations Accepted by American Universities.
- APA Style documented in Publications of the American Psychological Association.

> **Task 51 – Identify a dictionary, thesaurus, grammar book and a writer's handbook. List them here. Are there any other materials you may need for this phase of your research project?**

SOME WRITING ASPECTS

Technical papers are logically and coherently organized writings. No matter what kind of writing style you use, you need to make sure every section, paragraph, and sentence is directly related to your research topic. You also need to make sure all the components of the paper relate logically and that they are in some sort of order. For example, the introductory section can begin with a general description or thoughts about the research area and gradually get to the specifics. You can imagine it is like a funnel. It brings the reader from general materials to specific materials. It can also be compared to going to a new restaurant for a dinner. First you look for the general area, such as which city, county, and neighborhood. Then you get more specific and try to find the major highway, street and address of the restaurant. The next step is to get into the restaurant, select a table and order a few items from the menu—from general to specific.

Today, with the explosion of information, there are many researchers that I call Cut-and-Paste researchers. They read and Cut related materials and Paste them in a coherent and logical way for publications. They use cuts from so many different resources, authors and research areas that their final product is a new soup mixture, which they can claim as their own creation. There is nothing wrong about this approach. All I am trying to say is, if you build your skills by using this approach, you can conduct research and publish it too. Of course, there is more to research that intelligent compilation of the other people's work. Remember, a good portion of your research should be spent finding out what is already out there in a particular area. This is particularly true, if you are a novice researcher. There will be more about this in the next section.

At this time, I need to bring up two more important issues about writing. The first issue deals with the tense of the research report and the point of view of the paper. Almost all research uses the past tense. However, you may find that some writers use the present tense for special purposes. In regard to the point of view, in formal papers, the writer refers to herself in the third person, such as "the researcher," "the author," or "the investigator." If there is more than one author, the plural form of the above references may be used. The other issue to be considered is paragraph construction. Paragraphs have their own internal structure. They are like a micro version of a research paper. They should include a topic sentence, development sentences, and a concluding sentence. To make it simple, put a new description or thought at the beginning of the paragraph and then in a few sentences, provide more details, process steps, examples, cause and effect, comparisons, contrasts, compliments and/or critiques. These are a few of the techniques I use to develop my paragraphs. The last part of each paragraph must be the conclusion to all that has been said in the first part.

Just between you and me, I do not follow all these nice and logical guidelines to the tee. As you attempt to give a logical order to your research paper, you need to make sure it is not boring and dull for the readers. In this information-overload era, your writing must be interesting and stimulating enough to give you an "edge" over other writers. Remember, no one has an obligation to read what you have written. Your writing must keep the reader's interest so she will continue to read. Therefore, it is okay if you become creative and put some good "stuff," in the beginning, especially in the topic sentence, of each paragraph. Here are a few examples for you to read.

First example:

    The sense of presence that users
    experience in a virtual environment is
    perhaps the best-known attribute of virtual
    reality. It is an appeal to this sense of
    presence that is used to distinguish virtual
    reality as something different from merely a
    multi-media system or an interactive computer
    graphics display.

Second example:

Consistent with Piagetian thinking, research suggests that children's interactive experiences with computers provide opportunities for them to actively explore, test, create, invent new activities and observe the outcome of their efforts (Haugland & Shade, 1988; Schetz, 1994). Researchers postulate that when children have meaningful interactions with discovery-oriented, open-ended software, the computer becomes an important teaching tool.

Third example:

The primary purpose of this research was to carry out a study of the effectiveness of virtual reality on improving and maintaining learners' intrinsic motivation or interest. By providing virtual environments that stimulate curiosity, interest, and a sense of control, learners can be taught to generate their own motivational strategies. Since the virtual environment provides a sense of presence and intuitive interaction techniques, it may be possible to create scenarios to stimulate the learners' curiosity and interest.

Task 53 – Provide a brief paragraph that is in accordance with the recommendation covered in this section.

WRITING STYLE

As I mentioned before, the major goal of this book is to help you build research skills that are really necessary to become a good researcher in your field. It is important to select style guidelines for your communication with others. By communication, I mean the research reports that all researchers produce.

Although there are several different styles and formats for research, including theses and dissertations, I use the APA, which is the primary style used by the majority of the HCI community. Please remember, this section will be very brief and will cover the information you will need to get by. I have to say that, I do not consider myself an expert in the APA style. From time to time I refer to the APA Manual and if it does not make any sense, I may contact my colleagues for advice.

Task 54 – Find out who else in your university is familiar with the APA style and how you can get help from them.

RESEARCH REPORT COMPONENTS AND APA

In this section, I will briefly describe the components of a research report and give you several examples so you will be familiar with them. However, it must be noted that the next section of this book will cover each component in more detail. At that point, I will guide you through the draft version of your research report. Yes, you will get a second chance to deal with all of this in the next section.

Title Page

Title
A title is the briefest summary of the research report. It should be a concise form of your research topic and help the reader to grasp

the main idea of your research. This is an example: "THE EFFECTIVNESS OF VIRTUAL REALITY TECHNOLOGY IN THE TREATMENT OF PHOBIAS" This topic seems to be short but long enough to tell us what the research paper covers and interesting enough to make the reader want to know more about it.

According to APA, the recommended length of the title is 10 to 12 words. I recommend that the title have fewer words—5 to 7. Your title is the first thing your reader reads and if it is too long or boring, the reader will skip your paper and go to others. The title should be placed at the top of the page and centered.

Please pay attention to how the newspaper and magazine writers provide titles to their articles. I have learned a lot from them. I am sure that if you begin to pay attention, you will learn too. Please do not get me wrong. The media have a different purpose, which is to sell; however, it does not hurt to learn a few tricks of their trade. Whatever your title is going to be, get to the point.

Author's Name and Institutional Affiliation

The author(s) name(s) must be written starting with the first name, middle initial, and the last name. Although personal titles such as Ph.D., Ed.D., M.D., are not recommended, many publications insist on reporting them after the last name.

Running Head for Publication

An abbreviated title should not exceed 50 characters and should appear at the top right corner of each page of a published article. This running page is used for identification only. Please note that the running head for the title page will be placed at the bottom left corner of the title page. See the example below.

This is an example:

AN INNOVATIVE INTERFACE FOR
BROWSING THE INTERNET

Juliet M. Young, Ph.D.
Human-Computer Interaction Group
Clark Atlanta University

Running Head: Innovative Interface

Task 55 – Provide an example of a title page for a project. Make sure you include the title, author's name, institutional affiliation and running head for publication.

Abstract

An abstract is a brief image of the content of an article. In many cases that is all the reader will read. The abstract is also used extensively by abstracting and information services for indexing and retrieval purposes. Therefore, additional care and attention must be given to this section of the article.

According to APA, an abstract of empirical study should be between 100 and 120 words. An abstract of a review or theoretical article should be between 75 to 100 words. The major components of an abstract for an empirical study should include the following:

- The purpose of the study or the description of the problem under investigation.
- The subjects – Describe the number of subjects, type, sex, age and any other characteristics used for your study.
- The experimental method - Briefly describe the apparatus, data gathering procedures, complete names of the instrument(s) used and general procedures utilized.
- The results and findings – Include the information on the statistical methods applied to the data.
- The conclusions – Include the implications or applications derived from the study.

The review or theoretical articles takes the following form:

- The topic – Review in one sentence.
- The purpose, thesis, or scope of the article.

- The sources utilized – Give personal observations or review of literature.
- The conclusions.

Here is an example of an abstract:

Abstract

Objective: The primary purpose of this study was to investigate the effectiveness of the virtual reality technology in improving on and maintaining learners' intrinsic motivation or interest. Method: Eighteen undergraduate college students, 11 males and seven females, between 21 and 32 years old, served as subjects. The study employed objects as stimuli in the physical world and virtual world, which had to be manipulated and arranged in nine different patterns. Results: The data indicated a significance of difference between the subjects' performance in the virtual world and physical world with respect to curiosity, interest and sense of control. Subjects scored higher in the virtual world than the physical world in all measures. Conclusion: Researchers based on the analysis of the data concluded that virtual reality technology can stimulate learners' curiosity and interest, and heighten their sense of control.

Task 56 – Give an example of an "abstract" from a journal article of an empirical study. Please pay attention to the components of the abstract.

Introduction

In one or two paragraphs you introduce the problem of the study and provide the background by using the existing literature. Additionally, describe the logical relationship between the previous works and your current work. The last part of the introduction deals with the rationale for the study, what you did and why you did the study.

Please note that APA does not recommend using the "Introduction" as a heading. The description of the introduction should immediately follow the introduction and appears immediately after the abstract page.

An example:

Introduction

Virtual Reality (virtual environments) offers a new Human-Computer Interaction paradigm in which users are no longer simply external observers of data or images on a computer screen but are active participants within a computer-generated three-dimensional virtual world (Fontaine, 1992; Held, and Durlach, 1992; North and North, 1994; North et al, 1995a).

Consistent with Piagetian thinking, research suggests that children's interactive experiences with computers provide opportunities for them to actively explore, test, create, invent new activities and observe the outcome of their efforts (Haugland and Shade, 1988; Schetz, 1994). Researchers postulate that when children have meaningful interactions with discovery-oriented, open-ended software, the computer becomes an important teaching tool.

The primary purpose of this research was to carry out a study of the effectiveness of virtual reality on improving and maintaining learners' intrinsic motivation or interest.

Task 57 – Identify an example from a journal article and write down the summary of the "introduction" below.

Method

The method section describes, in detail, how you conducted the study. Sufficient details should be given so that other researchers can replicate your research. This section includes a description of participants or subjects, apparatus, and procedures.

Participants

Identification and selection of research participants is very important in terms of generalizing the findings and results to a larger population. All of the procedures for selecting a population and samples for your study must be described, in detail, in this section. In addition, it is important that you include the demographics of the participants such as the number of participants, gender, age, etc. Of course, depending on the investigation under study, you may need to provide the reader with additional information to clearly identify the subjects participating in the study.

APA has established ethical standards in using subjects, which must be followed and considered very carefully. More details will be provided at the end of this section. Additional information will be given in the next section.

Apparatus

You need to describe the apparatus and materials used to conduct the experiments. Remember, you need to provide enough information so that other researchers, if they choose, can replicate your research.

Procedure

Details, which describe each step of your research, should be included in the procedure section. You need to tell your readers, in detail, how you conducted your research.

An example:

Method

Participants

Eighteen Clark Atlanta University students, 11 males and seven females, between 21 and 32 years old, served as subjects for the study.

Apparatus

The virtual environment system for this study consisted of a Pentium-based Processing unit, a Stereoscopic head-mounted display (VRX, Virtual Systems Inc.), and electromagnetic 6D multi receiver/transmitter head-tracking device (FBS, Tracking Technology Corp.), And a steering device for navigating through virtual Environment. The VFRAM Virtual Reality Software and Libraries were used to create the virtual environment scene for this study.

Procedure

Each subject was given a demonstration of how to handle the materials used in the virtual world and was tested individually. The first experiment started with a two-block pattern. At each step, the difficulty was increased by increasing the number of blocks. The subject's score was based on a ten-point scale instrument administered at the end of each experiment. The scores ranged from very weak to very strong.

Task 58 – Provide an example of "methodology" from a journal article. If it is too long, write down the summary of each subsection.

Results

The results section describes the data collected and the statistical treatment of it in detail. Please remember, at this point, all you have to do is to tell the reader what data you collected and what statistical method was used to treat the data. You do not want to give a verbatim report of every piece of data you collected. Plan to provide your readers with a summary of the data and what it shows. In this subsection, tables and figures may be used. This will help to clarify your analysis of the data. Do not forget to number your tables and figures and label each with a caption. In addition, you need to reference each table and figure in your paper at the proper location.

An example:

> Results
>
> The subjective measures of the sense Of presence in the virtual environment increased gradually after each session while the subjective measure of sense of physical environment while attending the virtual environment decreased gradually across session. The results led to the conclusion that the longer subjects remained in the virtual environment the higher their sense of presence became, even though scenes were purposely created with a very low level of details.

Task 59 – Provide an example of the "results" section of a journal article. A summary will be sufficient for this purpose.

Discussion

At this point, you can begin to evaluate and interpret your results, draw inferences or generalize them for other situations and larger populations. At this point, you attempt to explain your contribution and how the study solved the problem you stated in the introduction subsection.

In this subsection, you may want to discuss the shortcoming of your study, any flaw and negative results, implications of the study, any suggestion for improvement and future research.

An example:

```
                    Discussion

     Although somewhat limited, the present
results are definitely important.  They attest
to the sense of presence experienced by subjects
in the virtual environment.  The degree of
anxiety and habituation observed would not have
occurred if the subjects did not immerse in
virtual environment.  With further research, it
is our belief that VED may well prove to be a
cost- and time-effective alternative to the
treatment of phobic disorders.
```

Task 60 – Find the "discussion" section of a journal article and write the summary.

References

At this point, I must remind you that, your research is as good as its references to other research in the field. You need to support your statements by referring to the literature you reviewed and documented in your paper. I simply use the author's last name and the date of the publication. The documentation is placed within the text and in the reference section of the paper. For example: (Smith, 1997).

Please be aware that you must reference any work you use in your paper. Make sure that all citations are listed in alphabetical order.

Here, I am going to briefly show you APA guidelines on referencing books and articles. For more detailed information, I suggest that you consult APA publication.

Books

Referenced books generally consist of four units separated by periods. These units are:

- *Author* – Write the last name, first name and middle initials. Place a comma after the last name. If there is more than one author, follow the same rule and place an ampersand (&) before the last author's last name.
- *Date* – Insert the date of publication in parentheses after the author's name followed with a period.
- *Title* – List the title of the book, capitalize only the first word, underline the entire title and place a period at the end.
- *Publication data* – List the city in which the book was published, followed by a colon, then list the name of the publisher, followed by a period.

A reference for a book by one author looks like this:

> North, M. M. (1996). <u>Virtual reality technology</u>. New York: Best Press.

A book with two or more authors will be referenced as:

> Roger, F. D., & Chen, K. L. (1974). <u>An introduction to artificial intelligence</u>. New York: IPS Press.

Smith, N. D., Jones, P. F., & North, M. M. (1997). <u>A guide to research</u>. Texas: Better Publishing.

Task 61 – Please provide a reference for a book with one author and a book with two or more authors.

Journals

When using articles, similar to the book referenced, capitalize only the first word of the title. The following examples will show how easy it is to reference a number of articles.

A journal reference with continuous pagination looks like this:

Robinson, M. D. (1995). Effect of virtual reality desensitization on the treatment of phobias. <u>Journal of Virtual Reality Environments, 46</u>, 121-128.

Please note that the volume number (46 in the above example) appears after the title of the journal and the page numbers appear after that.

A journal reference with separate pagination is written like this:

```
Kelly, F. G. (1997). Networking made
efficient. Journal of Computer Networking,
45(3), 54-61.
```

In the example above, the issue number (the issue number in this case is 3) is inserted within the parentheses immediately after the volume number of the journal.

A reference for an article from a conference proceeding will be documented like the following:

```
Varnner, F.D. (1996). A survey of medical
issues using virtual reality. Proceedings of
the Virtual Reality Medical Technology. (pp.
119-132). Nice, France.
```

Please note that (pp. 119-132) in the above example indicates the page numbers where the article is printed.

Task 62 – Please provide a citation for an article from a conference proceeding of your choice.

Popular Media

As you may recall, I strongly discourage the use of articles from sources other than referred journals. However, here is how you can reference monthly or weekly magazines, newspapers, and computer programs.

```
Ford, D. J. (1994, April). Virtual reality
therapy. Worldwide News,
pp. 56-59.
```

Please pay attention to the month and the date of publication for monthly publications. For weekly publications, you need to add the day of the month as well. For example: (1996, May 25).

A newspaper reference may appear like this:

```
Fresh, L. S. (1993, November 3). The next
personal computer was revealed. Madison
Journal, p. B8.
```

Computer Programs

The following example will show how to reference a computer program in APA style:

```
North, S. M. (1992). ProStat [Computer
program]. Atlanta, GA: Wizard Corp.
FMR-5667-Q34).
```

Task 63 – List a reference for an article from a newspaper of your choice.

> **Task 64 – Provide a reference for a computer program you may use for your research.**

QUOTATIONS

Quotes from any published materials whether it is yours or someone else's should be stated verbatim. The direct quotation must follow the exact wording and punctuation of the original material. This includes any mistake within the original published source.

APA guidelines distinguish two types of quotations, short and long. A short quotation has fewer than 40 words, any quotation longer than 40 words is considered a long quotation.

A short quotation is enclosed in double quotation marks. Longer quotations should be written in a free-standing block without using the quotation marks on a new line. Indent five spaces from the left margin. The quotation must be double-spaced. Indent the first line of any other paragraph within the quotation.

The following are examples of short quotations:

```
The researcher reported, "The effect of
visual queue on the client is much stronger
than auditory queue" (North, 1995, p.197),
```

but he did not specify the age of clients in the study.

Schemidt (1997) stated that "No matter what techniques you utilize to treat clients, your personal rapport has more positive effect in the outcome of the treatment" (p. 341).

Task 65 – Provide a quotation from an article or a book in the following space. Please check the recommendation for a short quotation in this section.

The following is an example of a long quotation:

Jones et al. (1985) reported the following:

Virtual Environments offer a new human-computer interaction paradigm in which users are no longer simply external observers of data or images on a computer screen but are active participants within a computer-generated three-dimensional virtual world. Virtual environments differ from traditional displays in that computer graphics and various display and input technologies are integrated to give the user a sense of presence or immersion in the virtual environments. Virtual environments also provide special techniques that allow users to interact with virtual objects. (p. 25)

Please note that when you use any direct quotation in your research paper, regardless of the length, proper credit must be given to the owner of the quotation.

All the quotations must have a complete reference citation. In any case, a written permission is needed from the copyright owner. Please note that the requirements to obtain permission are varied and you must investigate the proper process. Some copyright owners allow you to quote a short portion of their printed materials without a written permission. For example, APA allows up to 500 words to be used. Of course, you are required to give proper credit and reference of what you used.

Based on my own personal experience, the best policy to follow is to contact the owner of the copyrighted materials and find out what exactly they require you to do. Believe me. it is not that bad. All you have to do is ask.

GENERAL FORMAT

Your research paper should be printed on one side of a standard size paper, 8½ x 11 inch (22 x 28 cm). The paper must be heavy bond paper of a good quality.

Margins – All the top, bottom, right and left margins should be 1½ inch (4 cm) for every page. Normally, these margins are used by editors or reviewers to write their comments. Use left justification for the text—let the right margin be uneven.

Typeface and Size – You should use one of the common typefaces such as Times Roman, CG Times, or Courier and font size of 12.

Line Spacing – Double-space between all the lines of the text including the title, headings, quotations, references, figure captions, all parts of tables, etc.

Indentation – Leave five spaces at the first line of each paragraph, except the abstract, block quotation, titles and headings.

Page numbering – Place the page numbers in the upper right-hand corner of each page using Arabic numerals (e.g., 22, 75).

Spacing and Punctuation – Use one space after commas and semicolons. Use two spaces after colons, after the period at the end of each sentence, and after periods that separates elements of a reference citation.

Headings – Headings assist you in structuring and organizing your paper in a logical and professional manner that will help readers understand what you are presenting.

Although, the APA recommends the use of different heading levels for different kinds of articles, I will introduce you to a four-level heading system. The following are examples:

The first level of heading is centered uppercase heading.

VIRTUAL REALITY TECHNOLOGY

The second level of heading uses centered uppercase and lowercase heading.

Methodology

The third level of heading is written as flushed left, underlined, uppercase and lowercase heading

<u>Apparatus</u>

The fourth level of the heading will be in the form of indented, underlined, uppercase and lowercase paragraph heading ending with a period.

<u>Virtual Scene</u>.

TABLES, GRAPHS, AND ILLUSTRATIONS

Tables, graphs, and illustrations allow the researcher to present information to the reader which otherwise would have been either boring or exhaustive. Of course, there must be enough explanation in the text about each of the tables, graphs or illustrations to assist the reader in gaining a clear understanding of the research.

Generally, the illustrative materials should be as close as possible to their first reference in the text. However, because of the size of the illustrative materials, sometimes it is impossible to fit them in the same page immediately after the text. In this case, they may be placed on the next available page.

Illustrative materials should be given a number which follows the proper word, such as Table, which is in uppercase-lowercase followed with a period and the caption. All will be centered above the table. A caption is a concise description of what the table contains. The following shows examples of a Table and a Figure.

Table 1. Mean SUD Scores for experimental subjects for individual treatment sessions.

Treatment Session	Mean	SD
Ground level (0 meter)	5.66	0.74
Second floor (6 meter)	4.55	0.56
Fifth floor (15 meter)	3.45	1.34
Fifteenth floor (45 meter)	2.66	2.44

Figure 1. A line graph for heart rate and anxiety
level of experimental subjects across five
sessions.

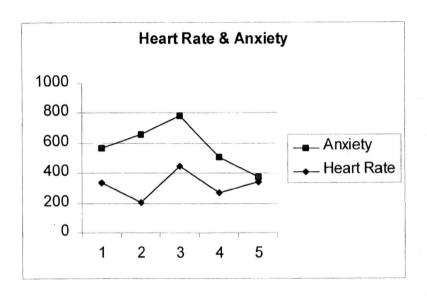

MORE ETHICAL ISSUES

It seems proper to introduce more of the ethical issues at this point.
Please note that when you conduct research, you need to consider
publishing your final product. We call this important step
"dissemination". Thus the ethical guidelines in this section are in-
line with our research process cycle. Of course, there will be more
detail about the dissemination of research in a later section.

The following is some additional information about ethical

guidelines which pertains to the subject. The information was written by and reprinted with permission from Dr. Justin Zobel.

Published Material

When submitting material for publication, researchers should:

- Ensure that results are accurate;
- Describe any limitations of experiments and any considerations that may have affected their outcome;
- Provide enough detail to allow other researchers to reproduce experiments, including (where relevant) method, sources of input data, and so on;
- Report the work of others fairly and accurately;
- Report relevant negative results as well as positive results;
- Avoid making deliberately misleading statements of any kind, or implying falsehoods.

The publication of multiple papers based on the same results is improper unless there is full cross-referencing. An example of cross-referencing is to refer to a preliminary publication from a more complete publication that is a later outcome of the same research. It should be made unambiguously clear to what degree the results are new. Simultaneous submission to more than one journal or conference of material based on the same results should be disclosed to all parties at the time of submission.

Other forms of self-plagiarism are currently the subject of debate. The conflicting positions are represented by two recent articles: "Copyrights and author responsibilities", H.S. Stone, IEEE Computer, 25:12, December 1992, pp. 46-51; and "Self-plagiarism or fair use?", by P. Samuelson, Communications of the ACM, 37:8, August 1994, pp. 21-25. The central issue involves whether it is acceptable to reuse your own text, even text describing background or principles (in contrast to text describing new research). The arguments are being conducted with regard to both copyright and ethics.

The issue is currently unresolved: however, researchers should be aware that some referees consider reuse of text to be unethical, on the grounds that a contribution can only be made once; even discussion of background or principles can present a new view of a topic that is itself a contribution to understanding research. The quality of such discussion is a factor in the decision as to whether the paper should be accepted. Moreover, any significant reuse of text by a researcher that is not explicitly referenced as a quotation can technically be regarded as plagiarism once the text has already appeared in a copyright form such as a journal or conference proceedings. The issue of how much text constitutes "significant" is open. Stone argues from copyright that reuse of two paragraphs or more is unacceptable; Samuelson argues from an informal survey of colleagues that, without specific permission, 30% of the paper being reused prose is "a gray area" and would recommend less reuse than that. He stated, "An informal survey of my colleagues suggested that perhaps 10% - one page of a typical conference paper - was a limit and that they would be uncomfortable recommending acceptance of a paper with more than that level of reuse, an exception being a journal submission that was a substantial expansion of a preliminary conference paper." Note that published text is the intellectual property of all of the authors, regardless of who actually wrote it. Researchers should avoid bringing themselves or their institution into disrepute, and therefore should not reuse text to a degree that is likely to be interpreted by a referee as plagiarism.

Any plagiarism of the work of others is unacceptable. Note that plagiarism is not limited to copying material from published papers. It also includes material in electronic form, such as technical articles made available on Internet or comments or suggestions made in e-mail. Gender-inclusive language - language that does not specify gender unnecessarily—should be used in all writing, including research publications.

Data related to publications should be made available for discussion with other researchers; however, any requirements of confidentiality in relation to data should be observed.

Authorship

The minimum requirement for authorship of a publication is participation in conceiving, executing or interpreting a significant part of the outcomes of the research reported. Note that this does not include subsidiary tasks such as implementation conducted under the direction of a researcher. Honorary authorship on any basis—seniority, "tit-for-tat", generosity, or coercion is unacceptable.

A researcher who has contributed to the research must be given an opportunity to be included as an author. There is no simple rule that establishes how much contribution to a paper is enough to merit authorship. Providing comments on a draft or two is almost certainly not sufficient; but conception in detail of the original idea almost certainly is.

On the other hand, a researcher should always be given an opportunity to be included as an author if their contribution has added to the quality of the paper sufficiently for it to be accepted by a more prestigious journal or conference than would otherwise have been the case. On the other hand, involvement in an extended project does not guarantee authorship on every paper that is an outcome of the project. In most circumstances, an author will have participated, to some degree, in every part of a publication, from the commencement or conception of the research to completion of the publication itself. A researcher who has only met the minimum requirements for authorship should consider choosing to be acknowledged instead, particularly when the researcher is a supervisor of the other authors. Co-authorship is a consequence of having made a genuine contribution to the intellectual property embodied in a paper. Simply being a student's supervisor is not sufficient to merit co-authorship.

A related issue is of author order, since many readers will assume that the first author was the primary contributor. A researcher who is clearly the primary contributor should be listed first. Where there is no obvious first author, possible approaches to ordering include: alphabetical or reverse alphabetical, with an explanatory footnote; a reversal or rotation of the order used on a previous paper by the same authors; choosing the first author based on considerations such as the value to each individual. An example of which would be a paper jointly written by a student and supervisor. The student should be listed first; or if all else fails toss a coin. The order of authors should always be explicitly discussed prior to submission, and be the joint decision of all the authors. A publication should contain due recognition of the contributions made by all participants in the relevant research. The work of research students, research assistants, and the assistance or advice of colleagues should be properly acknowledged. Acknowledged persons should, if the presence of their name could be interpreted as their endorsement of the contents of the paper, be given the opportunity to read the paper prior to submission.

Any groups or organizations that funded or contributed significantly to the research should be acknowledged. Where, for example, the address of an author is not the institution that employed them while they conducted the research, the institution should be acknowledged explicitly.

The issue of authorship is discussed further under "Supervision" section.

Supervision

When a researcher supervises a post-graduate or honor student, the student undertakes a research program under the supervisor's direction, culminating in a written report that is assessed. Often material in the report is the product of joint research, and must be explicitly acknowledged as such. However, if the research or report is substantially the work of the supervisor, the student is in breach of University regulations if the work is submitted as their own. As far as possible, supervisors should ensure that the work submitted by research students is the work of the student, and that the research is valid.

It is improper for a supervisor to publish a student's work without giving appropriate credit (usually authorship) to the student. In the event a supervisor is enrolled in a research degree, the supervised project must be distinct from the supervisor's research. For example, an honor student should not subsequently be incorporated into the supervisor's assessed work.

Published work that is generated during the course of a post-graduate degree is often jointly attributed to both student and supervisor. Frequently, the student has undertaken the bulk of the task of capturing some idea in text, conducting experiments, and creating the paper that that describes the idea. However, it is also usually true that the paper would not have existed without ongoing input from the supervisor, and moreover the conception and initial development of the idea is often due to the supervisor. In these cases student and supervisor should both claim authorship. This practice of shared authorship does not diminish the student's final work, and it acts to prevent the supervisor from limiting their responsibility to the student and to the quality of the research.

There are also cases in which sole authorship by a student is appropriate, such as during the latter stages of a candidacy when the student can be expected to be in contact with other experts in the field, and is by then an expert. Good Ph.D candidates should be able to prove themselves toward the end of their candidacy by conducting largely unassisted research. Supervisors should encourage their students to write a paper of which they are the sole author—that is, to develop an idea, conduct experiments and write a paper with minimal input. They should give them the freedom to do so. In such cases, the supervisor should be consulted prior to submission.

Under no circumstances should supervisors use their position to force a student to include them as an author. A supervisor who has only minimally met the requirements for authorship should consider choosing instead to be acknowledged. Additionally, a supervisor should not assume that they are automatically an author of a student's paper. Authorship should always be explicitly discussed. Disputes over authorship should be raised at the earliest opportunity and taken to the research coordinator or the head of department if they cannot be resolved amicably.

A supervisor, and in particular the senior supervisor on a supervisory team, is responsible for ensuring that the student has reasonable access to resources necessary for their project, and that the academic aspects of the program proceed steadily and at a sufficient rate. Supervisors must ensure that research students are aware of ethical guidelines such as those described in this document.

Refereeing and Examination

These guidelines are adapted from a resolution passed by the Transactions Advisory Committee of the IEEE Computer Society. Researchers should not referee a paper or examine a thesis where there is a real or perceived conflict of interest, or where there is some reasonable likelihood that it will be difficult for the referee to maintain objectivity.

- A paper (or thesis) by an author with whom the referee has recently been a co-author
- A paper by an author in the same department as the referee, or in a closely related department either at the same university or at another university with which the referee is closely associated
- A paper by an author who was a recent student or supervisor of the referee
- A paper by an author with whom the referee has had recent close interaction, including not only personal relationships but also antagonistic interactions such as competition for an appointment

In such cases, the referee should notify the editor that an alternative referee should be sought. (The editor will appreciate the referee suggesting possible alternatives.) Where there is no alternative referee, the editor may request that the referee evaluate the work despite the conflict. In such cases, assuming that the conflict is not so severe as to prohibit objectivity, the referee may evaluate the paper but the referee's report should carry an appropriate caveat.

Referees should respect the confidential nature of the papers they referee. Such papers should not be shown to colleagues, except as part of the refereeing process. They should not be used as a basis for the referee's own research or for the referee's personal gain. Referees should not indicate whose papers they have been reviewing or the outcome of the review process. In some cases, that the authors have already made the work publicly available, for example on the Internet. In which case, the publicly available version does not have to be treated in a confidential manner. When a referee recommends acceptance of a paper, the referee is assuring the technical content, originality, and proper credit to previous work to the best of the referee's ability to judge these aspects. A referee should not recommend acceptance if the paper is not of adequate standard in some respect. The onus is on the referee to take sufficient care to fully evaluate the paper. Referees who are not able to assure the quality of the paper should not recommend acceptance without an appropriate caveat.

Referees should make every effort to complete reviews in a timely and professional manner. Reviews should be constructive. For example, Knuth has remarked that on several occasions, he has been able, in the review process, to correct a proof or generalize a result and thus strengthen the paper anonymously on behalf of the author. Rejections should clearly explain, not only the faults of the paper, but a process that the author might use to produce a more acceptable outcome. Even in the case of a paper that a referee believes to be totally without contribution, it is helpful to explain how the author might verify whether this evaluation is correct. Every paper, no matter how weak, should have a careful and thorough review. Active researchers should, as a consequence of the peer review system, referee two to three times as many papers as they write. Researchers should only decline to referee a paper with good reason.

Task 66 – Summarize the ethical issues introduced in this section and bring it to class for discussion.

SECTION FOUR

❧ ☙

A GENERIC RESEARCH APPROACH

Congratulation, you have made it to this point! Now that you have done the skill-building tasks, you are ready to do that interesting research project. I told you that you would make it! I realize that it was not an easy task. As a matter of fact, the last chapter got on my nerves and went very slowly. But, if we want to produce that winning research project and publish it for the world to read, we need to follow some guidelines.

In this section you will put the draft of your research project together step by step, using a generic research approach or template. Please note that I have covered all the topics related to the research process in the previous sections. This section will briefly repeat what I have said before. The primary purpose of this chapter is to help you remember what you are supposed to do in and teach you how to do it in an organized fashion.

I am also trying to move you along so that you will be exposed to a more formal and intellectual definition of research components. To do this, I am going to introduce you to the materials offered at the graduate school level. These materials are usually produced for graduate students to help them deal with theses and dissertations. I do not expect you to write a thesis or dissertation at this time; however, I want to give you a brief overview of theses and dissertation guidelines. This will assist you with your research paper, required for the current course you are taking.

Do not panic! I think you are ready and with the preliminary work you have done, it should be "a piece of cake." And, remember, your advisor is always willing to assist you. I am there for you too! Lets start! I am excited already! Aren't you?

You must have access to a computer with a good word processing package. I am currently using Microsoft Office 97™, which includes Word 97™ word processing. Whatever software you are going to use, it is time for you to learn it and learn it well. Go ahead and set up a workspace with the configuration I gave you in the pervious section about APA style and formatting. After doing the task in this section, you should enter them into an electronic file in your computer.

By prompting you with that "Task Box," you will be asked to conduct your task in this section. As soon as you encounter it, you need to conduct that portion of the research. It has been intentionally organized in sequential fashion for ease of learning.

To assist you further, I will provide excerpts from one of my own research papers in each subsection. These excerpts, all of which come from the same research, should provide you with additional examples, which you may use as models for your research. I have also provided a sample research paper in Appendix A, which uses the APA style. As a final note, please remember that you need to use the present tense at the proposal stage. After conducting your research, and as the situation requires, you may change to the past tense.

TITLE PAGE

This page covers information about the title of the research, the author's name, institution affiliation, and the running head.

An example of a research title page:

A NOVEL USER INTERFACE FOR INFORMATION

EXPLORATION AND VISUALIZATION

Max M. North and Sarah M. North

Human-Computer Interaction Group

Clark Atlanta University, Atlanta, GA 30314

Max@acm.org, Sarah@acm.org

Running Head: A Novel User Interface

Task 67– Create the title page for your research paper by using the information provided in this section and the pervious sections.

ABSTRACT

An abstract is a brief version of the article. In general, it includes the purpose of the study, methodology, results, and conclusion. It should not exceed 100 words.

An example of an abstract:

Abstract

Objective: The primary objective of this study was to investigate the design, implementation, and evaluation of a graphical user interface prototype, called InfoVis, for exploration of databases. Method: The prototype InfoVis interface was designed, developed and implemented on a Sparc Sun Workstation. Subject (n=20) were randomly placed in an experimental group (n=10) and a control group (n=10). To access the performance of the InfoVis, the subjects from both groups were presented with ten different queries to perform using InfoVis and a traditional SQL respectively. In addition, to ensure the usefulness, effectiveness, learnability and attitude of the interface, several usability tests were conducted. Results: The results indicated that there exists a significant difference between the performance of the experimental group and the control group (t=2.69, df=18, p<0.05). Conclusions: The InfoVis interface showed superior performance over SQL for each task performed by the experimental and control group.

Task 68 – Write a brief 100 word abstract. Please remember that all the components must be placed in one paragraph.

INTRODUCTION

This section introduces the topic and provides a brief overview of your research. It should emphasize the importance of the topic and the crucial need for conducting the research at this time. You will introduce the purpose of your study and explain how your research study is grounded in the current research literature. Typically, the introduction section contains the following subsections:

- Statement of the Problem
- Purpose of the Study
- Research Questions
- Significance of the Study

Statement of the Problem

A problem statement should clearly establish the specific issue of your research and demonstrate that the problem is worthwhile and relevant to the information technology area. This statement should be given in a very clear manner.

You should also provide sufficient information regarding the background of the problem you are addressing in your research study. Additionally, a brief description of how the problem evolved to its current state should be given. A paragraph should be sufficient.

It is also important to remember that the main reason for conducting research should be justified by providing a linkage to the current state-of-the-art research activities in the area. At this point, you may justify your proposed research by referencing the work of others in the area under investigation. A few paragraphs should be sufficient at this point.

A brief statement of the problem:

Statement of the Problem

Generally, information exploration of
databases is performed using query languages. Most
query languages such as Structured Query Language
(SQL), are based on relational algebra or calculus.
While relational algebra and calculus provide a
powerful means to formulate and specify queries,
their usage is an extremely tedious and complex
task (Cha, 1990), (Mayhew, 1992), (North & North,
1993), (Nowell et al, 1993), (Zloof, 1975) for
computer users, especially for *naive* users. In
addition, query languages are redundant in the
sense that the same query may be expressed in many
different ways (Kim et al, 1988). In fact,
empirical research indicates a wide variation in
response times in the implementation of different
query languages.

This research argues that providing a graphical
visualization of the databases, queries, and search
results will empower users with the complex task of
information exploration (Ahlberg et al, 1992), (Cha,
1990), (Johnson, 1992), (North & North, 1993),
(Nowell et al, 1993), (Sarker & Brown, 1992). To
provide and enhance graphical visualization, a new

Multiple attribute presentation widget called *dynamic slider* is introduced (North & North, 1993). The *dynamic slider* enables the user to present multiple value ranges rather than a single or anchored value to minimum or maximum points.

The primary objective of this study was to investigate the design, implementation, and evaluation of a graphical user interface prototype, called InfoVis, for direct manipulation of databases. This prototype information exploration and visualization interface allows users to explore a database with graphical widgets such as a novel *dynamic slider*. Specifically, the InfoVis interface enables the user to search a database without the need to create or formulate complex syntactical query statements. The *dynamic slider* and other widgets are utilized to assist users in mental visualization and representation of objects and actions.

Task 69 – Write the statement of your problem. Please remember that a few paragraphs will be sufficient.

Purpose of the Study

The exact intent of the research should be indicated in this segment. A few sentences will be sufficient to show the purpose and objectives of the research.

An example of the purpose of a study:

```
                    Purpose of the study

        The purpose of the study was to investigate the
   design, implementation, and evaluation of a prototype
   graphical user interface which will allow the user to
   directly issue queries that may be either difficult or
   impossible when utilizing the traditional query
   languages.  This novel information exploration and
   visualization interface provides users with graphical
   widgets to explore a database.
```

Task 70 – It is time to write the purpose of your research study in a concise manner.

Research Question(s)

Research question(s) should be produced for each of the specific inquires of the research. The question(s) must be direct, brief and concise.

An example of a research question:

```
                    Research Question

     Compared to the traditional Structured Query
     Language, would the novel user interface (InfoVis) be
     effective for information exploration and
     visualization of databases?
```

Task 71 – Specify the concise statement of your research question. It is okay if there is more than one research question.

Significance of the Study

The significance of your research should be documented in this section. Basically, it should demonstrate how the findings of your research will effect current knowledge of the research area. It should also indicate the impact your research will have on the information technology area. In general, this section should provide the potential of your research outcomes. The need for the research must be clearly emphasized.

An example of how to document the significance of a study:

Significance of the Study

This research is expected to contribute significantly to the existing body of knowledge on direct manipulation of the databases using the novel InfoVis interface. The InfoVis interface provides better and faster learning tool for building queries to explore the databases. In addition, advances made on *dynamic Slider* widget and *Dynamic Frames* has far more benefits for many applications of information explorations and visualization.

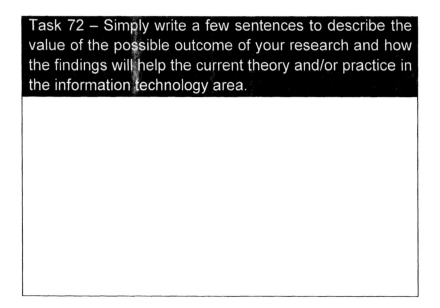

Task 72 – Simply write a few sentences to describe the value of the possible outcome of your research and how the findings will help the current theory and/or practice in the information technology area.

REVIEW OF THE CURRENT LITERATURE

In general, a review of the literature will indicate your level of knowledge and understanding of the issues that have been previously researched in your particular area. It should begin with a brief introduction to demonstrate the scope and nature of the review and the way it is organized. Here are the different aspects of literature review:

- Organization of the Review
- Analysis and Synthesis of the Literature

Organization of the Review

There are many different ways to organize the research reviews. You need to choose one and follow it. Please recall that I recommended that you to start from the general and go to the specific. This is a very good technique for novice researchers.

Analysis and Synthesis of the Literature

The researcher needs to critically review current related literature in the area of her interest. The researcher also needs to report the similarities, contradictions and interrelationships among the articles reviewed with clarity and conciseness. The literature review must demonstrate the researcher's awareness of current research activities and show how the reviewed literature built the base for her research.

An example of a partial literature review for a study:

Literature Review

The literature review for this study consists of two major components. The concept of *dynamic slider* as a novel multi attributes widget is briefly reported here. The second component is the implication of *dynamic sliders* widget within the frames and clusters which is reviewed and discussed in detail.

Dynamic Slider As A Novel Multi Attributes Widget
Traditionally, sliders have been used as a metaphor to assist the user in entering either a single value or a single range value anchored to minimize maximize points of a field. The concept of dynamic queries (Ahlberg et al, 1992) has been extended so that the users can implicitly construct complex queries by utilizing visual and graphical techniques and tools

---

such as *dynamic sliders* (North & North, 1993). By
utilizing *dynamic sliders,* InfoVis interface is able to
represent dynamic range(s) rather than a single or
anchored value to provide the mechanism for assisting
the user in formulating more complex queries. The use
of novel *dynamic sliders* widget distinguishes the
InfoVis interface from other database interfaces.

Dynamic Sliders Widget Within Frames And Clusters
       Frames were introduced in the mid-1970's by
Minskey to present knowledge. Since then, the
Minskey's frame concept has been extensively utilized
by other applications, such as databases (Minskey,
1988). Simply, frames are structured forms of
attributes (Gupta et al 1991), (Leong et al 1989).
One of the advantages of the frame is that users do
not need prior knowledge of the attributes for an
object (Gupta et al, 1991), (Koh & Chua, 1989). In
essence, frames reduce the burden of typing and
eliminate need for user knowledge of acceptable
attribute values. Frames also provide several other
advantages. The default values of attributes may be
explicitly stated (Koh & Chua, 1989); however it may
be possible to set a default for other query interface
(e.g., SQL) but a user has to memorize the specific of
the default. Frames also provide for consistent
placement of attributes. This visual consistency
Should ease the task of understanding sets of
attributes. On the contrary, SQL or natural language
does not enforce a consistent ordering of attributes.
Finally, frames can be graphically and visually

extended to allow for building more complex queries. Frames with all of the advantages appears to be static and bounded to the specified attributes values thus allowing the user to set attributes that are totally depended on the widgets capabilities used within a frame. The *dynamic slider* utilized within the frame extends the power and characteristics of the frame from a static state to a dynamic state. This new dynamic state of the frame, called *dynamic frame* allows for more efficient use of the frames and possibly combines several static frames to one dynamic and more general specifications and constrains of the attribute values.

Clusters have been introduced and successfully utilized in VIMSYS query interface for image databases (Klinger et al, 1993). Klinger, et al, define the clusters as follows: "Clusters are abstract query structures which encapsulate any combination of query objects. A cluster is simply a box with a user-provided natural language label." In general, clusters possess the following characteristics and can be: (i) linked to other clusters, or frames; (ii) expanded to reveal their contents; (iii) modified for customization; (iv) moved around the screen; and (v) retrieved, saved, grouped, renamed, or removed. Clusters reduce the burden on the user for manipulating groups of attributes. Specifically, clusters reduce any group of attributes into a single unit with a customized natural language label, such as: "Aircraft query base on range of external fuel"; or "Aircraft' performance at high altitude."

Since the label is customized as chosen by the

user, it will provide a better cue for recalling and
constructing more complex query rather than
remembering and interacting with several frames and
set of attributes at a time. Clusters also provide a
mechanism for the user to graphically manipulate while
forming queries. Moreover, the small size of the
clusters allow more manageable and meaningful
information such as frames and other clusters to be
displayed on the same screen (Klinger et al, 1993).
Clusters contribute extensively to the domain of
module reusability. Clusters may be retrieved and
combined together to form a new query. These
characteristics of clusters increase the efficiency of
formulating especially complex queries. Finally,
clusters are linked via a specific attribute. This
limitation will enhance the user's understanding by
simplicity of the link element. For more detail
information of clusters the reader may refer to the
work of Klinger, et al at UIST '1993 (Klinger et al,
1993).

Clusters power also may be extended by the dynamic
nature of the dynamic frames it represents. In other
words, clusters inherent the properties of the frame
or frames that are within them, called *dynamic
clusters,* and in turn frames inherent the properties
of *dynamic sliders* within themselves. This hybrid
architecture gives birth to the new interface for
exploration and visualization of information. The
basic block of the *dynamic sliders* empowers the frames
and clusters which empowers the user for facing the
challenges of graphically forming complex queries with
a very low cognitive load.

. . .

Task 73 – Here is where you need to provide the summary of your literature review, the analysis and synthesis of at least five approved research articles. You may need to consult with you advisor on this matter.

Note: Use additional paper to complete this section of your research paper.

THEORETICAL FRAMEWORKS

In general, a theoretical framework is needed to guide the researcher through the course of the study. As the experimental designs incorporate the theoretical framework, it may not be a necessary component of the qualitative studies.

It must be noted that the theoretical framework is introduced to present and define the dependent and independent variables and their interaction in a particular situation.

Please remember the brief discussion in an earlier section, which reported that experimental research is one of the best frameworks available to the researchers. I, as well as many other researchers involved in information technology, recommend a wider exploration and usage of this research method. The major components of theoretical frameworks are as follows:

- Independent and Dependent Variables
- Null Hypotheses
- Limitations of the Study
- Technical Terms

Independent and Dependent Variables

Precise situations or events that the researcher predicts are called independent variables. They predict the impact that they will have on the dependent variables. In other words, dependent variables rely on the independent variables. Researcher should clearly define the research variables in this section.

The researcher should also document the relationship which, she predicts will, exists among the variables. This can be further illustrated by using diagrams to demonstrate the variables and how they relate to each other.

An example of research variables:

```
          Independent and Dependent Variables


     The independent variables in this experiment were
the interfaces that subjects utilized to build
queries:  (i) InfoVis interface; and (ii) SQL
interface.  The dependent variables were:  (I) time to
build query in order to get the desired output; and
(ii) usefulness, effectiveness, learnability, and
attitude.
```

Task 74 – Please describe the independent and dependent variables you are using in your research. Please ask for help. It is okay to ask!

Null Hypotheses

The null hypothesis is a formal statement that predicts the relationship among the independent and dependent variables in the form of what is not expected to happen (i.e., there is no statistically significant difference between the current interface usability and the proposed interface usability for the virtual reality development software).

An example of a null hypothesis for the study:

```
                    Null Hypothesis

        The major null hypothesis was that, there would be
    no significant difference between the performance of
    subjects who use InfoVis interface and the subjects
    who use the traditional SQL interface.
```

Task 75 – The null hypothesis should be described at this point. Please remember, the null hypothesis shows what is not expected to occur. Again, ask for help, if you need.

Limitations of the Study

The researcher should indicate any areas she cannot control or present any limitations of the study. For instance, when subjects are used in the study, the researcher must make the assumption that all the subject's responses are truthful and accurate.

An example of the study limitation section:

Limitation of the Study

This study was confined to undergraduate and graduate students currently enrolled at Clark Atlanta University. The study involved a population of 20 students. Generalizations from the findings of this study should be limited to situations that do not differ significantly from the situations in this current study. The instruments of this study were of a self-reporting nature, thus, the validity of the data was dependent upon the attitude, honesty, and accuracy of the participants' responses.

Task 76 – Here is where you document any assumption or limitation of your research study. A short paragraph will be sufficient.

Technical Terms

The researcher must define and explain all the technical terms used in the research. Note that you do not need to define the terms widely used in the information technology area.

METHODOLOGY

The methodology section of the research investigation should describe, in detail, how the study was conducted. The researcher must provide sufficient details to allow replication of the study by other researchers, if they desire to do so. The following are the most important components of the research methodology section:

- Research Design
- Subjects
- Using Human Subjects
- Site and Setting
- Apparatus
- Instrument(s)
- General Procedures

Research Design

Basically, the design of the research indicates which type of research the researcher intended to conduct. Although there are a variety of research designs, the researcher must clearly and adequately document it in this section.

An example of a research design:

```
                        Methodology

Research Design

        This research study used two major research
designs.  The first research design was a theoretical
research approach to the design of a novel interface
and the second was the traditional experimental design
to evaluate this interface.  This experiment compared
two different interfaces for query building for
databases.  The first interface was InfoVis, briefly
described above.  The other interface was SQL, the
traditional query building interface.
```

Task 77 – Simply determine the type of research design you are going to use for your project and describe it in a short paragraph.

Subjects

A clear and concise description of subjects' identification and selection for the study must be provided. A brief demographic summary of the selected subjects is written in this subsection. If the research design requires several groups of subjects, these groups must be described precisely, particularly the procedure for assigning them to each group. In any case, subjects must be voluntary participants in the research.

An example of a description of subjects in general:

Subjects

   The experimental subjects were twenty individuals (n=20) who were randomly selected for this study from the students who currently enrolled at the Clark Atlanta University. Ten subjects were placed in the experimental group and ten subjects were placed in the control group. A typical subject was 18-23 year-old (76%), and female (72%). In addition, the prior data collected from the subjects revealed that subjects' skills vary from novice to expert with novice users (subjects) dominating the population.

Task 78 – Provide a brief description of how subjects will be identified and selected for your research project. If you use groups, describe each.

Using Human Subjects

The researcher must ensure that no harm will come to the subjects of her research. In addition, the researcher must make arrangements to secure the confidentiality and anonymity of subjects and any information related to them.

A formal permission from your institution is required. You also need to secure a signed consent form which describes the purpose of your study and all the procedures to the subjects.

An example of a consent form used for a research project:

Consent Form

The purpose of the study is to investigate the design, implementation, and evaluation of a prototype graphical user interface which will allow the user to directly issue queries that may be either difficult or impossible when utilizing the traditional query languages. Individual responses and scores will be kept completely confidential. The student's names will not be associated with test scores in any way. Feedback on the general results of the experiment will be available upon written request.

I have read the above information. I have had ample opportunity to ask questions about the procedures, and I agree to participate in this study. I feel that I meet the requirements for this study. I am aware that my participation is voluntary and I may withdraw at any time without penalty.

Signature_____ Age_____ Gender_____ Date _____

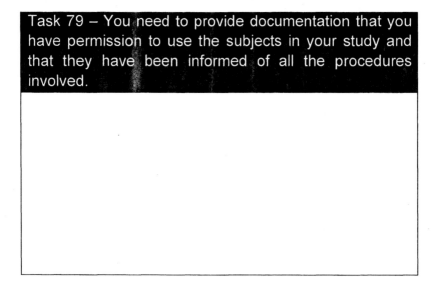

Task 79 – You need to provide documentation that you have permission to use the subjects in your study and that they have been informed of all the procedures involved.

Site and Setting

The researcher must clearly identify and describe the physical location that will be used to conduct the research. This setting may be your own institution or more specifically, a laboratory within the institution.

An example of a description of a research setting:

<u>Site and Setting</u>

The site of this study was Atlanta, a large metropolitan city in the Southeast. Atlanta is the home of the Atlanta University Center (AUC), the largest consortium of historically African American

Institutions of higher learning. Clark Atlanta
University, one of the six AUC institutions, was the
targeted institution.

The study was conducted in the Human-Computer
Interaction Laboratory of the Computer and
Information Science Department.

Task 80 – A brief description of the physical location of the place you conduct your research should be documented here.

Apparatus

The researcher should describe, in detail, all the apparatus and materials needed to conduct the research. Please remember that you have to provide sufficient information for other researchers to be able to replicate your work, if they desire to do so.

An example of an apparatus description:

<u>Apparatus</u>

     The apparatus for this research study consisted of a Sparc Sun Workstation™. The software was developed in-house by advanced undergraduate students under the direct supervision of the principal researcher.

Task 81 – At this time, you need to describe all the apparatus and materials you used in your research.

Instrument(s)

Instruments are tools for measuring and collecting data for the research study. All of the instruments used in the study must be described very precisely and clearly. The description of the instruments should include information about the creator, reliability, validity, etc. In this section, it is a good idea to cite other research that has used the same instruments. This will provide additional justification for the use of the instrument.

An example of a description of an instrument:

Instrument

Evaluation of the prototype system is critical to ensure the quality of the final product. To determine the desirable characteristics and features of the InfoVis prototype, a comprehensive survey was conducted.

In the second phase, an instrument consisting of ten different queries based on an Aircraft database was designed. These queries started with a simple query and gradually became more complex. For instance, the subjects were given the following queries:

- Find aircraft(s) that have service ceiling of 60,000 Feet and above.

- Find aircraft(s) that have speed at high altitude of Above mach 2.16 or equal; and take off run of 1,300 Feet; or rate of climb at sea level above 40,000 feet.

- Find aircraft(s) that have range of the external fuel Between 3700 km and 4,800 km.

Task 82 – Please indicate the measurement instruments you will use and give a brief description of them.

General Procedures

In this section, the researcher must describe, in detail, steps taken to conduct the research. These steps include subject identification and selection, apparatus used or designed, any computer programs developed, any prototype designed and implemented, all procedures involved in conducting the experiment, collection and analysis of data.

An example of a description of general procedures:

General Procedures

The first phase of the study concentrated on the theoretical research, and eventually, the design and development of the InfoVis interface prototype. Several evaluations were performed on this prototype. The prototype development and its evaluation were tightly interleaved. Each prototype was evaluated in realistic settings, and the outcomes was accommodated in the design of the next prototype, thus ensuring quality improvement during each stage of system development. In summary to ensure usefulness, effectiveness, learnability, and attitude of the InfoVis interface prototype, several usability tests for each intermediate prototype design was conducted (Mayhew, 1992).

In the second phase of the study, twenty students were randomly selected for this study. Ten subject were placed in the experimental group while other ten were placed in the control group. Each group was given an overview of experimental procedures and a short instructional period primary to acquaint users with the domain subject and interfaces. The subjects from the experimental and control group were presented with ten different queries on an Aircraft database and the mean time to complete each task utilizing SQL and InfoVis interfaces were collected.

Task 83 – Please describe the general procedures you will use to conduct your research.

RESULTS

The results section describes, in detail, the data collected and the statistical treatment of it. All the statistical tools needed to analyze the data must be selected and described, in detail. Of course, the selection of a certain statistical procedure over another, may be a difficult task for novice researchers and sometimes even for more advanced researchers. It is my recommendation that you consult literature and/or experts in the field.

The statistical tools will assist the researcher in making decisions with a level of significance for either accepting or rejecting the research hypothesis. To demonstrate the outcome, you need to provide appropriate tables of various analyses of your data. You may use figures to further illustrate the main effects and interaction between your study variables.

The outcome of the data analyses allows the researcher to present the findings of the study. Additionally the outcome allows her to provide possible answers for research questions.

An example of statistical usage and general results:

```
                      Results

      The data were subjected to appropriate
  statistical procedures.  These procedures included
  a measure of central tendency, and the t-test.  The
  result of the t-test indicated that there exists a
  significant difference between the performance of
  the experimental group who used InfoVis interface
```

And the control group who used traditional SQL
(t=2.69, df=18, p<0.05). Please see Table 1.

Table 1. Means, Variance, Standard Deviations, Degree
of Freedom, and t-test of subjects in experimental and
control group.

	Experimental Group InfoVis Interface		Control Group Traditional SQL		Analysis Df (18)
Measure	Mean	SD	Mean	SD	t-test
Performance Queries	170.01	58.93	266.20	96.71	2.69

The null hypothesis was not confirmed.
Therefore, the results showed the superior
performance of the nfoVis interface over SQL
interface for each task that was performed by
experimental and control groups.

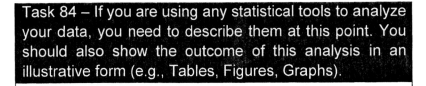

Task 84 – If you are using any statistical tools to analyze your data, you need to describe them at this point. You should also show the outcome of this analysis in an illustrative form (e.g., Tables, Figures, Graphs).

Note: Use additional paper to complete this section of your research paper.

CONCLUSIONS, IMPLICATIONS AND RECOMMENDATIONS

In this section, the researcher reports what was found and interprets the findings of the research. The researcher also describes how these findings can effect the state of current research and possibly the state of current developments in the field. Implications and recommendations should follow the conclusions.

Conclusions

Based on the findings of the study, the researcher can drive conclusions, interpret and explore the meaning of the research findings.

An example of a conclusion:

Conclusion

Using twenty subjects, several testings of the interface have been performed, and the InfoVis interface is now being tested with larger populations and more complex queries. Further prototyping and testing will improve the overall performance of InfoVis interface. Although we have built several prototypes to test out the ideas, the work is still in its early stages. InfoVis interface is an ongoing project with Clark Atlanta University's Human-Computer Interaction Group. The preliminary results of the pilot study ($t=2.69$, $df=18$, $p<0.05$) so far are very

encouraging, and users' feedback is positive.

Task 85 – Show what you can conclude from the findings of your research. What is/are the answer(s) to your research question(s)?

Implications

This section includes the implications or what the researcher can infer from the results and their implications for the current state of research in this area.

An example of implications:

```
                        Implications


        The InfoVis interface is an operational prototype

    though functionally quite a simple system.   In other

    words,   the preliminary results so far are very

    encouraging,  and users' feedback has been positive.

    In essence, the empirical results demonstrate that

    InfoVis interface appears to be a promising approach

    over traditional SQL techniques.
```

Task 86 – Write what you infer from your study and what the implications of your findings are.

Recommendations

Based on the findings, the researcher should report any recommendation that may indicate an improvement in the theory, research or development. This section will allow the researcher or others to follow-up on current research or replicate the research in an improved fashion.

An example of recommendations:

Recommendations

    This is only a prototype of InfoVis interface, and many significant problems must be resolved. For instance, graphical meta structures provided to the user at this time is build by database designer and administrator, further work must be undertaken to allow the user to build this initial stage of the interface. At this point the number of links between the databases is limited to one link. Additional investigation is needed to provide the user with the mechanism for multiple linkages.

Task 87 – Please document the recommendation you made, based on the findings of your research study.

DISCUSSION

The researcher should document an evaluation and interpretation of the results in this section. This will allow the researcher to generalize the results for another situation or population. Any shortcoming, flaw or negative results may be introduced here.

An example of discussion:

Discussion

As the system is used over time, many *dynamic frames* and *dynamic clusters* will be stored in the library. Libraries may be tagged private or public depending on the person who creates it. Eventually, the number of *dynamic frames* and *dynamic clusters* in libraries either private or public will increase and re-using these stored *dynamic frames* and *dynamic clusters* will become increasingly difficult (Klinger et al, 1993). Also, each dynamic frames or dynamic clusters may have different versions with different attribute sets that may add to the problem at hand. An Object (refers here to *dynamic frames* and *dynamic clusters*) Management Interface will be needed to assist users in manipulation of objects in the libraries. The *dynamic slider* concepts have been applied to the relational database at this time. Thus, the effect of *dynamic frames* and *dynamic clusters* on other type of databases, such as hierarchy and network databases are not tested yet. Finally, the major shortcoming of the current study is that there were no comparison between the InfoVis interface with two or more graphical interfaces to find out if there are any significant differences among their performance or not.

Task 88 – Write a brief paragraph to introduce any issues that relate to the discussion section.

REFERENCES

The reference section or bibliography covers an alphabetical list of all published and unpublished articles, books, theses, dissertations, or manuscripts, cited in your research paper. The reference list must not contain any item not cited in the body of your research. In addition, all the reference formats must adhere to the APA guidelines and style, as mentioned in the pervious section.

An example of the list of references:

References

Ahlberg, C., Williamson, C. & Shneiderman, B. (1992).
    Dynamic queries for information exploration: An
    implementation and evaluation. Proceedings of
    ACM CHI'92 Human Factors in Computing Systems
    Conference. (pp. 619-626).

Cha, S. (1990). Kaleidoscope: A cooperative menu-
    guided query interface (SQL version).
    Proceedings of IEEE Artificial Intelligence
    Applications. (pp. 304-310).

Gupta, A., Weymouth, T. & Jain, R. (1991). Semantic
    queries with pictures: The VIMSYS model.
    Proceedings of the 17th International Conference
    on Very Large Data Bases.

Johnson, B. (1992). TreeViz: Treemap visualization of
    hierarchically structured information.
    Proceedings of ACM CHI'92 Human Factors in
    Computing Systems Conference. (pp. 369-370).

Kim, H. J., Korth, H. F. & Silberschatz, A. (1988).
    PICASSO: A graphical query language. Software-
    Practice and Experience. 18, 169-203.

Klinger, J., Swanberg, D. & Jain, R. (1993). Concept
    clustering in a query interface to an image
    database. Proceedings of UIST '93. (pp. 11-21).

Koh, T. & Chua, T. (1989). On the design of a frame-
    based hypermedia system. Hypertext II.

Leong, S., Sam, S. & Narasimhalu, D. (1989). Towards a visual language for an object-oriented multi-media database system. Visual Database Systems. North Holland Publishing.

Mayhew, D. J. (1992). Principles and guidelines in software user interface design. New Jersey: Prentic-Hall & Simon & Schuster: Englewood Cliffs.

Minsky, (1988). The society of mind. Simon & Schuster: Englewood Cliffs.

North, M. M. & North, S. M. (1993). *Sarah:* An information exploration and visualization interface for direct manipulation of databases. Proceedings of Graphics Interface '93 Conference. (pp. 163).

Nowell, L. T., Hix, D. & Labow, E. D. (1993). Query composition: Why does it have to be so hard? Proceedings of East-West International Conference on Human Computer Interaction. (pp. 226-241).

Sarkar, M. & Brown, M. (1992). Graphical fisheye views Of graphs. Proceedings of ACM-SIGCHI'92 Human Factors in Computing Systems Conference. (pp. 83-91).

Zloof, M. M. (1975). Query-by example. Proceedings of National Computer Conference, AFIPS Press. (pp. 431-437).

Task 89 – Here is the last task for completing your research paper! Make a list of all the references used in your research.

MORE ADVICE

You did it! Congratulations to you and your advisor. As you may know, it is not very hard to do research as long as you follow some kind of guidelines.

At this point, you need to use your word processing package, type what you have prepared and submit it to your advisor for review. And, please, do not get defensive, if your advisor returns your final report with comments and corrections on it. Actually that is a good sign! You simply thank your advisor and follow her recommendations for corrections and resubmit it. If there are any comments or corrections that you do not understand, you need to discuss them with your advisor. And, again, remember, your advisor is there to assist you by critiquing your work, it is her responsibility to mention all your weaknesses to you so you can grow. Good Luck!

At this time, I do recommend that you read the next two sections of this book. The following section will help you to understand how you can possibly publish your work. The final section will introduce a unique future perspective on information technology.

PUBLISHING YOUR WORK

Are you ready to publish your work? Yes, you heard me right. If you have taken my advice and followed me up to this point, why not follow through and continue to pursue your work so that it can be published? There is no guarantee that your work will be selected for publication, however, it is imperative that you submit your research paper to the professional journals for review and possible publication. That is the only way you can get feedback from professionals.

Depending on the journal, the acceptance rate may range from the top 20% to 40% of all the submitted and reviewed research reports or what is called, at this point, the *manuscript* or simply the *paper*. It is still a good idea to get feedback from the people who review this sort of research. There is no charge for it and there is nothing to lose.

SELECTING A SCHOLARLY PUBLICATION

The things I taught you about regarding how to choose a scholarly article for your research will apply to the selection of a scholarly publication to submit your work to. As a reminder, make sure the publication is a refereed reviewed publication.

Your next question is probably, "How do I find a publication to submit my paper to? Generally, all the journals have a "Calendar of Events" section or a section with a similar title. This section lists the upcoming conferences and "call for papers." You should read this section and do a brief investigation of the announcements to understand what kind of papers they are looking for and then proceed. Believe me, there are a lot of announcements that will keep you busy for days and months just trying to follow-up on them.

No matter which of the publications you select, find out what the subject(s) are or what the general theme is of the papers they publish. It is important to know if their papers are in the same subject area as your interest. Simply find out if there is a match between their interests and yours. It is also a good idea to call them or to send them an E-mail. Get as much information as you need to feel comfortable about what the publication is looking for. I always ask the publication for the guidelines and format for publishing with them. You also need to get this important information before you begin to prepare or submit a paper.

The following is a brief example of a few conferences that look for research papers:

> July 19-23, 1998: *VR and Training conference*, Atlanta, GA. Contact vrt@cyber.edu, FAX: 404-233-5676.

> August 6-11, 1998: *Computer and You*, Nice, France. Contact monique@sophia.fr, FAX: +33 97633 22.

Note: The two examples were given to show you what the announcement might look like. I made them up for the purpose of demonstration. So, don't contact these two!

Task 90 – Find a "Call for Papers" from one of the ACM journals or the IEEE journal and rewrite it in this box.

SUBMITTING THE MANUSCRIPT

You need to read their guidelines and format requirements very carefully. Some publishers, or I should say editors, will return your manuscript if you do not follow their instructions. It is very important that you follow directions because some publishers will simply ignore your work if it does not follow the prescribed format. If you do not comply, you could be sitting in your rocking chair, waiting for a reply to your submission, forever.

In general, guidelines discuss what kind of research papers they accept, what format and style they require. You are lucky if the publisher's format adheres to APA. If this is not the case, and the publisher has other specific requirements, you must follow them to a tee.

The following is a sample of guidelines for a "Call for Papers." Guidelines and formats vary among the publishers. All you have to do is to obtain a copy, read, comply and submit.

This is an example of guidelines and a format for the author of a research paper, partially reprinted, with permission, from the International Journal of Virtual Reality (IJVR).

AUTHORS' GUIDE

CONTENT

The IJVR solicits original manuscripts with possible multimedia enhancements and software for publications, including articles on original research and applications in all areas of virtual reality. This includes scientific discoveries, technical developments, innovative applications, proposed or newly adopted standards, social issues, reports, book reviews, reviews of new hardware and software, and artwork using the VR medium. The appropriateness to publish a submission shall be based on what professionals in the virtual reality field want to see in such a journal, as judged by the content editor in charge of the manuscript, following the guidelines of the Editorial Board.

REFEREEING

All materials submitted for publication, including invited papers, are refereed to ensure adherence to originality and quality standards as well as to ensure a broad enough interest among readers of the journal. While the IJVR is published with an emphasis on multimedia, the printed portion must be self-contained in the sense that it provides all the important points and results. The printed edition will be the primary focus of the refereeing.

CONTENT EDITOR
...

ORIGNIALITY

...

ARTICLE LENGTH

...

TITLE AND AUTHOR NAMES

...

ABSTRACT AND KEYWORDS

....

Note: As you may have noticed that the publisher provides you with a complete detailed set of information you may need to submit your manuscript.

Task 91 – Request guidelines and a format from a selected publisher. List the title of the publication and bring it to class to show to your advisor and classmates.

GET YOUR PAPER ACCEPTED

This title may be misleading. All I am trying to say is, do all you can to get your paper accepted. It is very simple! Follow, follow and follow the guidelines and format. Of course, I am assuming that you completed all the tasks you were given in this book and that you have conducted an excellent and high quality research project.

If you have done what I have suggested, there is a good chance that you will get some feedback from the publisher an/or editor. Normally all the accepted papers in any journal go through several revisions. You may receive a long official letter or E-mail message pointing all the weakness and needed improvements in your paper. Do not panic! Just do as they say and provide them with what they ask for. They are just trying to help you develop a quality paper for their readers.

Another suggestion is to find out if the journal accepts short papers. The main reason for this is that, the kind of the research you conduct at the beginning of your career is not very extensive and is usually conceptual research, research-in-progress, or research with preliminary results. Sometimes it is easier to get into this category than into others because it is easier, at this stage of your research, to get a good match between the publisher and your goals.

CRITICISM AND YOU

If your paper is totally rejected with criticisms that you cannot bare, please remember, you are not alone. All of the other people who were not a part of that 20% to 40% got rejected too! So what? I must to tell you; some of the best papers are papers that were first rejected, the author rewrote them and resubmitted the manuscript with major modifications. This is okay, as long as there is not a major flaw in your research. Of course, since you are conducting relatively simple and straight-forward research, you should not have any problems with the backbone of your research.

The moral of this story is, if your manuscript was rejected, rewrite and resubmit it. You should resubmit your research to the same publisher. You should also attach a letter of thanks to the reviewers and the editor for their constructive comments. Additionally, you should ensure the editor that, to the best of your ability, you did what you were told to do.

You should also be aware of the emotional factors involved in research and especially in publishing the research. Do not allow the criticisms to get on your nerves. Use the criticisms in a positive manner and remember, all criticisms help you grow.

PUBLISHING IN THE POPULAR PRESS

Even though you have gone through a lot of trouble to publish your research, the professional journals have a limited number of members who may or may not read your research paper. As a matter of fact, there are so many publications that it makes it very hard for anybody to read, even a small portion, of the articles. I read a few articles from a few selected journals. Other researchers, like me, are so busy with their own research that they do not have time to read what they select from their favorite journals. Do not be surprised if, even after publication, your paper has to compete with many of the other papers to gain the attention of the readers. You want to inform as many people as possible about your research. In which case, you may want to use the popular media as well as the professional publications.

To have your work published in the popular press, you need to prepare a *news release* of your research. I have provided a sample of a news release and a few instructions in this section.

It is also important to know that publication of your research in the popular press is a service to the community. It is very important to let others know about your research. It is your responsibility to let others know what research you are conducting and why. At a minimum, you are helping to expand the public's knowledge about your area. The following is an example of an actual news release for one of my own research projects.

NEWS RELEASE

FOR IMMEDIATE RELEASE

May 8, 1997

VIRTUAL REALITY COMBATS FEAR OF PUBLIC SPEAKING

The fear of speaking is often cited as the world's most common social phobia. This communication disorder is frequently identified among the top five most prevalent phobias of any kind. It does not appear to be limited by age, gender, economic or educational variables. Until this time, traditional treatment has included systematic desensitization, cognitive restructuring and skills building. Current advances made through the use of computer display technology and the work of researchers in Atlanta and Boston is responsible for the creation of virtual reality technology for use in treating the fear of public speaking and other psychological disorders. In Atlanta Dr. Max M. North, Dr. Sarah M. North and Dr. Joseph R. Coble are pioneers in Virtual Reality Therapy. Their technical advancements have been combined with the work of Dr. Dennis Becker of THE SPEECH IMPROVEMENT COMPANY in Boston. Research is being conducted in the Virtual Reality Technology Laboratory at Clark Atlanta University. This is the first known controlled study of the effectiveness of virtual reality therapy in the treatment of subjects who suffer from fear of speaking. Additional support was provided by US Army Research Laboratory, and Boeing Computer Services.

This first of a kind collaboration of cutting edge technology and time tested traditional treatments is producing far reaching benefits which will have a positive impact on clinical and non-clinical treatment sessions for sufferers of the fear of public speaking. Additionally, the general population will benefit from virtual reality research as this new technology provides a safe, confidential and economic approach to the treatment of psychological disorders.

Current plans are to expand the research to a wider population and to extend the test site at the Virtual Reality Technology Laboratory in Atlanta to THE SPEECH IMPROVEMENT COMPANY offices in Boston. This will allow for the first known application of virtual reality therapy technology in a non-laboratory controlled setting with measurement in the real world.

Subjects who participate in the research are recruited from Clark Atlanta University Introductory Psychology classes. Following an extensive two-stage screening process, subjects are selected from the pool. They are assigned to two treatment conditions: virtual reality therapy and a control group. Subject speakers are placed in front of a virtual auditorium which gradually fills with virtual people. Simulation of room and crowd noise, including laughter, commentary and applause is created and experienced as part of the treatment sessions. The treatment schedule consists of eight weekly sessions. The sessions last 10 – 15 minutes. Based on current success records, alternative treatment regimens are being considered.

The symptoms experienced by the subjects during virtual reality therapy mirror those which most speakers experience during a speech to a town meeting or presentation at a business conference. They include an increase in heart rate, lump in the throat, dry mouth, sweaty palms, loss of balance, weakness in the knees, etc..

This study of the fear of public speaking indicates that virtual reality therapy is very effective in reducing self-reported anxiety. The virtual reality therapy treatment results in both a significant reduction of anxiety symptoms (SUD and ATPS measurements) and the ability to face the phobic situations in the real world. Treated subject speakers now report the ability to speak comfortably in front of a crowd with better confidence.

Research for treating phobia through the use of virtual reality began at Clark Atlanta University in 1992. Many studies have been made by the virtual reality treatment research team. In 1996, the team was awarded the prestigious CYBEREDGE Award for the best virtual reality project of the year.

CONTACT: Dr. Max M. North
Virtual Reality Technology Laboratory
Clark Atlanta University
Atlanta, GA 30314
Telephone: (404) 880-6942
Email: max@acm.org

Task 92 – Prepare a short news release for the research you just conducted and submit it to the media, after you have secured permission from your advisor.

CHAPTER SIX

✍ ✎

A LOOK INTO THE FUTURE OF INFORMATION TECHNOLOGY

In this last chapter my co-author, Dr. Richard A. Blade, has been given an opportunity to describe what you are going to experience in the next few years when it comes to information technology, and to speculate about more futuristic concepts. Hopefully this will give you an opportunity to think more philosophically about your future, and will provide food for classroom discussion.

Currently you have a telephone and probably some form of cable television and (at least at the campus) access to the Internet. Provided on the Internet is email, newsgroups where everyone can express their opinion about the particular subject that group deals with, chat rooms for real-time interaction with others, ftp for sending and receiving computer files, telnet for checking into remote computers, such as those containing the catalogs of major libraries, and finally, the World Wide Web, where anybody and everybody publishes private and personal information about everything one can possibly imagine.

But technology is rapidly promoting changes. The first change we are going to see is an integration of the phone, the TV, and the Internet. In five to ten years (depending on your location) your home will have a single cable and a single company providing all those services and more, with a single "information services" bill provided each month.

First, you will have videophone (already available on the Internet) replacing the telephone. No, you won't have to let anyone see you naked or in hair curlers. You can switch the viewer to a "stock" photo of yourself.) You will have a "whiteboard" on which you can write or draw pictures to show the person you are speaking with. "Teleconferencing" and telecommuting" will become increasingly more common, permitting a significant fraction of the population to work out of their homes, and live wherever they wish—whether it be a South Pacific island or in a secluded cabin in the Rocky Mountains. Rush hour traffic might be largely eliminated, and large cities might not attract so many people as they do now.

You can, of course, watch TV as you do now, but you will also have "video on demand"where you can "pay-per-view" anything you currently obtain through a videotape rental store. More importantly (but a few years later) you will use a "head mounted display" (HMD) so you can view movies in ultra wide angle, much as you see in the IMAX or OMNIMAX theaters today. Moreover, your HMD will permit full stereographic viewing, giving you a real sense of distance and depth.

The Internet, and in particular, the World Wide Web, will change the most. Even now, Web browsers are beginning to appear that translate the text on a Web site to other languages. Foreign language will pose no problem in the future, as all browsers will not only be able to format the text content in any desired font and size, but in any language as well. All the World's literature will be available in all languages.

And navigating on the Web won't be in two dimensions as it is today. You will be able to navigate in three dimensions, doing a "walkaround" of an object or a "walkthrough" of a building, clicking on three-dimensional icons to link you to other three-dimensional worlds. Even today we have a primitive form of this in so-called "VRML": virtual reality modeling language.

Electronic games will be played with full "kinesthetic" inputs, giving the player the full experience of motion with a "motion platform" as well as "motion tracking" so that as the eyes or head move, the picture and sound are adjusted accordingly. The result will be true "immersion": making it hard to distinguish the "virtual" experience from the "real" experience. This is the so-called "virtual reality" that exists in only a very primitive form today.

The applications of the virtual reality technology will be countless. Let me just tell you about one: surgery. In the future I predict that almost all surgery will be done "endoscopically" and with "telepresence". That is, the patient will be prepared for the surgery in the local hospital, but the surgeon will be in a remote location, perhaps half way around the World, in something that might resemble an airplane cockpit, observing and controlling the surgical cutting, suctioning, and burning tools inside the patient's body. If the surgeon is removing cancerous tissue, for example, he or she can twist a knob to color that tissue red, so that it can be visually distinguished from the healthy surrounding tissue. In fact, it is not clear that the image the surgeon sees will even be an accurate representation of what is being "seen" by the video camera. Surgeons today are discovering that a device moved up the aorta can be more easily be maneuvered around a corner into a branch vein if the surgeon only sees a simplified drawing rather than the full photographic representation.

The libraries of today will be gone. Instead, all the World's books will be available for reading online. Of course you exclaim "I would HATE to read a book from a computer monitor. I want a book that I can hold in my hand and turn the pages." If you INSIST, you can simply print out a copy of the book, either a chapter at a time or the entire book. Most likely, however, is that you will discover that a HMD will give you what you want.

But let me now go further into the future and speculate on what lies ahead. We will discover that electronic information translated into sounds, pictures, and feelings for our senses to detect is inefficient and not very effective. Instead, the information will be fed directly into nerves to the brain that will create the illusion of the sensory data. Similarly, a person will only imagine moving his or her arms or running. The data will be taken directly from the brain and fed into the computer. Think this is far fetched? I have already seen a working model of the nerve-computer interface that will accomplish this! It is easy to see how the "holideck" displayed in "Star Trek: The Next Generation" can be built.

Of course when one starts extrapolating from these concepts, it is natural to start asking questions like "Will it be possible someday to have an artificial brain composed of wires and transistors instead of nerve cells?" If so, it might be that the brain would be in one location, like a large computer room, while the body would be merely a robot that transmits sensory information to that location, and receives information from that location as to how to move its muscles.

And how do you know that that is not the situation right now? How do you know that your thinking processes are not taking place at a remote location and that your body is merely a robot that transmits and receives to that location. Perhaps the brain does not "think" at all! Perhaps it is merely the "radio transmitter/receiver". People whose religious views are of a "universal consciousness" can probably subscribe to this, but is there any SCIENTIFIC evidence that might support such a radical conclusion?

Remarkably, the answer is YES, though it is far from conclusive. Let me first quote the enigmatic mathematical theorem knows as "Goedel's theorem" or "Goedel's proof". That theorem, having a long, rigorous proof, states that it is impossible for a system composed of discrete objects like nerves or even atoms or nuclei, no matter how numerous, to come up with mathematical theorems that human beings can think up. No matter what mechanism we ascribe to the thinking that goes on in the brain, we always come to the conclusion that it MUST be discrete. Thus IF we accept Goedel's theorem as correct, we inevitably come to the conclusion that human thinking cannot be confined to the brain.

The field of quantum physics provides an equally enigmatic bit of evidence. The mathematical formalism of quantum physics predicts that the KNOWLEDGE about certain kind of atomic processes causes certain physical effects. That is, consciousness affects reality.

Moreover, it predicts that the effect is INSTANTA-NEOUS, violating the law of relativity theory that nothing, neither objects nor signals, can travel faster than the speed of light. Until about 1960 it was widely accepted that this was a flaw in the quantum theory. However, in 1960 a man by the name of Bell proposed "Bell's theorem" that provided a method of testing the phenomenon. Remarkably, all the experiments to date have supported the fact that in the quantum theory consciousness does, in fact, affect reality.

At this point it becomes clear that the astronomer Eddington was right: "Nature is not only stranger than we suppose, it is stranger than we CAN suppose." I leave it to you, the student, to think about these concepts and imagine the future. To catalyze thinking and initiate some classroom discussions I provide a few exercises.

Task 93 – Suppose that to read an electronic book, you were given a head-mounted display. Describe what characteristics it would have to have for you to find it acceptable. When appropriate, provide actual QUANTI-TATIVE characteristics, such as the number of degrees in the field, width (the angle the open book makes with the eye) and the resolution in dots. (Hint: Recall that an ordinary VGA computer screen has 640 x 480 dots. Recall also that about 1980, when a TV was used as a computer monitor, there were only 40 characters in a line across the screen.)

Task 94 – Suppose you were have the kind of job you would like following your college education. Would it be possible to telecommute? If so, what kind of equipment would you require to accomplish it?

Task 95 – Videophones and videoconferencing now exist on the Internet, but the pictures displayed are small and somewhat jerky. What do you think has to be improved in order to remedy these limitations? Would "compression" of the electronic information help?

Task 96 – Since about 1970 it has been possible to have some blind people "see" by connecting a video camera to a mat placed on the person's back. The light areas in the camera image are transmitted to mild "shockers" at corresponding locations on the back, and the person "feels" the picture from the camera. Do you think the person interprets the image in the same way as a person who sees through their eyes? A person who is born blind is not helped with this high-tech aid. Why do you think that so? Currently there is talk about a hand-held device that transmits information to the person through a rapid sequence of small electrical shocks. What do you think the limitations of such a device are?

Task 96 Continues

Task 97 – When you want to understand a person's personal views of aratheresoteric or philosophical nature, it is often easier to ask a simple question associated with a contrived hypothetical situation. Here is an example: Suppose that someday we can travel by a method that I shall call "body reconstruction". To travel to Mars, you would lie down under a huge machine that would determine and make a blueprint of just how the various atoms and molecules are put together in your body. It would then put that information on a laser beam, or some other method of transmitting information and send it to Mars. There, another machine would use the blueprint to reconstruct your body with a supply of atoms and molecules there. Out of that machine on Mars walks a true clone* of "you". It has your memory, your senses, your physical appearance. But to consider this traveling and not cloning, your now obsolete body back on Earth needs to be destroyed. Question: First, do you accept that this method is scientifically possible? Second, if this method of travel were available to you, would you use it? As a matter of interest, in 1970 I took a poll of scientists at Caltech, two of which were Nobel laureates. What do you suppose the results of the poll were? Assuming the answers were both yes, what does this say about the person's view of their identity, or "soul" if you wish?

Task 97 Continues

Task 98 – Scientists no longer consider "causality", which says that time flows only in one direction, a sacred principle. Suppose you were to go backwards in time to before you were born and shoot your mother. Does that mean you would immediately disappear? Do you believe in precognition, that is, a person receiving information from the future? If so, does that mean that, by using that information, it is possible to change the future?

Task 99 – Subliminal images can be flashed on a screen that transmit information into the subconscious mind without any conscious awareness. It is illegal for movie theaters to advertise concessions using this technique, but certain movies have made use of the technique to increase the emotional impact. How do you think this could be used as a learning tool?

Task 100 – An avatar is a computer graphic creature that represents a person on the computer screen. It can be made to move its lips with yours and to follow your motions in other ways as well. The classroom of the future might have a person at home, who sees the class as a group of avatars through a HMD. Describe an avatar that you might use to represent yourself and tell why you chose what you did. It is certainly possible to change avatars as easily as changing pants or a dress. Would you like to change avatars frequently, or would you prefer a "stable" image for others to view you?

Task 101 – Planaria, or flat worms, have the characteristic that the genetic material of the food they eat is not destroyed in the digestion process. In a famous experiment researchers trained planaria to respond to certain lights to get their food. Then they ground up the trained planaria and fed them to other planaria, who acquired the ability without training. What does this say about storage of memory, at least in the case of planaria? Do you have any reason to believe this relates in any way to humans?

APPENDIX A

This appendix provides reprint of a complete research paper published by The International Journal of Virtual Reality, Volume 3, No. 3, 1997 (with permission).

VIRTUAL REALITY THERAPY:
AN EFFECTIVE TREATMENT FOR THE FEAR OF PUBLIC SPEAKING

Max M. North, Sarah M. North, and Joseph R. Coble
Virtual Reality Technology Laboratory
Human-Computer Interaction Group
Computer & Information Science Department and
Department of Psychology
Clark Atlanta University, Atlanta, Georgia, 30314
E-mail: Max@acm.org, Sarah@acm.org, jrcoble@prodigy.net

Abstract

<u>Objective</u>: The major goal of this research was to investigate the efficacy of virtual reality therapy (VRT) in the treatment of the fear of public speaking. <u>Method</u>: After an extensive two-stage screening process, sixteen subjects were selected from the pool. They were assigned to two treatment conditions: VRT (N=8) and comparison group (N=8). Fourteen subjects completed the study. The VRT group was exposed to the virtual reality public speaking scene while the comparison group was exposed to a trivial virtual reality scene and guided by the experimentors to manage their phobia either by using visualization techniques or self-exposure to the situation they feared. The VRT and comparison group sessions were conducted on an individual basis over a five week period. Two assessment measures were used in this study. The first measure used was the Attitude Towards Public Speaking (ATPS) Questionnaire. The second measure used was the eleven-point Subjective Units of Disturbance (SUD) scale. These measurements assessed the anxiety, avoidance, attitudes and disturbance associated with their fear of public speaking before and after treatments. In addition, objective measures such as heart rate was collected in each stage of the treatment. <u>Results</u>: Significant differences between the six subjects who completed the VRT sessions and comparison group were found on all measures. The VRT group showed significant improvement after five weeks of treatment. The comparison group did not show any meaningful changes. <u>Conclusion</u>: The authors concluded that VRT was successful in reducing the fear of the public speaking.

Introduction

The fear of speaking is often cited as the world's most common social phobia. This communication disorder is frequently identified among the top five most prevalent phobias. It does not appear to be limited by age, gender, economic or educational variables. Until this time, traditional treatment has included systematic desensitization, cognitive restructuring and skills building. Current advances made through the use of computer display technology and the work of researchers (authors) in Atlanta and Boston is responsible for the creation of virtual reality technology for use in treating the fear of public speaking and other psychological disorders. This research was conducted in the Virtual Reality Technology Laboratory at Clark Atlanta University (CAU) and with technical assistance of The Speech Improvement Company in Boston. To the best of our knowledge, this is the first known controlled study of the effectiveness of virtual reality therapy in the treatment of subjects who suffer from the fear of public speaking.

Research into this widespread phobia was conducted through the collaboration of CAU, the U.S. Army Research Laboratory and Boeing Computer Services, with special technical assistance from the Speech Improvement Company, Inc. With the assistance of the Speech Improvement Company, the research will have a positive impact on the clinical sessions of subjects suffering from the fear of public speaking. Additionally, the general population will benefit from the virtual reality research because the new technology provides greater access to a safe, confidential and economical approach to the treatment of psychological disorders.

The subjects' anxiety and avoidance behavior were interfering with their normal activities. They were unable to participate in the social gatherings, classes, or professional conferences. The symptoms experienced by

the subjects during virtual realty therapy included an
increase in heart rate, feeling a lump in the throat, dry
mouth, sweaty palms, loss of balance, weakness in the
knees, etc. These symptoms also appeared in the studies
which dealt with the treatment for acrophobia (fear of
heights), agoraphobia, and fear of flying.

Similar to our first known controlled studies of
VRT, the study of the fear of public speaking indicated
that VRT was very effective in reducing self-reported
anxiety. The VRT treatment resulted in both a significant
reduction in anxiety symptoms, as measured by SUD and
ATPS, and the ability to face the phobic situations in
the real world. At this time, several of the subjects can
comfortably speak in front of a crowd with confidence.

The idea of using virtual reality technology to
combat psychological disorders was first conceived in the
Human-Computer Interaction Group at CAU in November 1992.
Since then, the first known pilot studies in the use of
virtual reality technologies in the treatment of
agoraphobia have been conducted. This includes an
investigation of the use of virtual reality for specific
phobias: fear of flying (North & North 1994), fear of
heights (Williford, Hodges, North & North, 1993;
Rothbaum, Hodges, Opdyke, Kooper, Williford & North,
1995; North, North & Coble 1995b) and fear of being in
certain situations such as a dark barn, an enclosed
bridge over a river, and the presence of an animal, such
as a black cat in a dark room (North, North & Coble
1995a; 1996a; 1996b). Other researchers have realized the
potential of virtual reality in the treatment of
psychological disorders. These contemporary research
activities have established a new paradigm that is
attracting serious scientists from the computer science,
psychology, and medical fields. The present study sought
to extend the previous work to include a larger number of
subjects and a wider range of psychological disorders.

Method

Subjects

Subjects for the research were recruited from introductory psychology classes at Clark Atlanta University. A group of thirty-five undergraduates underwent and extensive two-stage screening process to ensure that they were suffering from the fear of public speaking and had no other serious physical or psychological conditions. The participation of all subjects was strictly voluntary.

The first stage of the screening process consisted of a set of questionnaires administered in the psychology classes. The questionnaires contained items that screened students for the fear of public speaking consistent with the diagnosis of a specific phobia (American Psychiatric Association, 1994). The questionnaires excluded subjects with panic conditions and other specific disorders, including substance disorders, major medical illness including thyroid disease, and the use of medication with significant psychotropic or physiologic effects. Additional screening criteria included in the questionnaires was symptom duration for at least one year and strong motivation for overcoming a phobia.

The second phase of the screening process involved a more stringent diagnostic procedure. It included a clinical interview and completion of the modified Attitude Towards Public Speaking Questionnaire (Abelson and Curtis, 1989). Subjects having symptoms limited to the fear of public speaking, a social phobia and consistent with the diagnosis of a specific phobia were included in the study. During this phase, subjects also completed a questionnaire regarding various demographic variables which included sex, geographical region, rural vs. urban, socioeconomic status, experience with computers, computer games and/or virtual reality.

The remaining subjects were assigned to two treatment conditions: virtual reality therapy (VRT) (N=8), and a comparison group (N=8). The two groups were as closely matched as possible with respect to demographic and severity of symptoms. In order to minimize the confounding variable of treatment expectancy, informed consent for treatment statements were obtained after the group assignment. After the first set of assigned measures, the comparison group subjects were informed that they would undergo repeated testing at the end of the five weeks. They were exposed to the trivial virtual reality scenes and advised by the experimentors to manage their fear and expose themselves to the situations they were avoiding. This approach was used to offset the placebo effects. The comparison group was not treated with a systematic treatment program. All subjects in the two groups were asked not to communicate with other subjects and not to self-treat with any relaxation after exposure to the phobic situation. All subjects were asked to keep a diary of any new medication regimens, including over-the-counter medications, caffeine use, significant stresses, and new illness and/or treatment.

Assessment Measures

The screening questionnaires used in this study assessed several inclusion and exclusion criteria. DSM-IV criteria for specific phobia (i.e., fear of public speaking, avoidance of feared situations, belief that the fear is excessive, interference from fear), desire for treatment, desire to participate in a treatment study, presence of panic attacks, history of panic attacks, and presence of claustrophobia were assessed by this instrument.

This **Attitude Towards Public Speaking Questionnaire** (ATPS) contains six items that assess attitudes toward the fear of public speaking. It is adapted from Abelson and Curtis (1989) with modifications that relate to the fear of public speaking. The following dimensions, rated on a 0-10 semantic differential scale: good-bad, awful-nice, pleasant-unpleasant, safe-dangerous, threatening-nonthreatening, and harmful-harmless are included.

The **Fear Questionnaire** was constructed for use in this study. The Marks and Mathew' (1979) Fear Questionnaire which assesses the degree of distress experienced from the fear of public speaking was also used. The four situations that subjects were exposed to were speaking in an auditorium without any audience; speaking in an auditorium with audience; speaking to an audience who talked to each other and did not pay attention to the speaker; or speaking to an audience who laughed at them. Each of these categories were varied by the size of the audience, ranging from 0 to 100. The situations were rank ordered and rated based on the level of discomfort produced. This determined the most appropriate use of the VRT.

Reactions according to a modified version of the **Subjective Units of Disturbance** (SUDS) scale were collected every few minutes during exposure on a 0 (no discomfort) to 10 (panic-level anxiety) scale (Wolpe, 1969). This is a very quick and simple measure of anxiety. The method has been used widely and been shown to correlate well with objective physiological measures of anxiety (Thyer et al, 1984).

The instruments used in the pilot studies were of a self-reporting nature. The validity of the data depended on the attitude, honesty, and accuracy of the participants' responses. Current literature regarding virtual reality research recommends the use of physiological data (e.g., heart rate, blood pressure, galvanic skin response, EEG/EMG, etc.) to measure the sense of presence, perception of physically being in a virtual world. For more information on sense of presence in virtual reality, readers may refer to the references

listed in this article. For instance, Barfield addresses
this issue and writes that techniques which measure sense
of presence typically and primarily involve subjective
assessment, which is most useful for initial exploration
and hypothesis generation (Barfield and Weghorst, 1993).
Barfield's hypothesis is that as sense of presence
increases within a virtual environment, the participant
should experience physiological changes that can be
measured and analyzed to determine the optimal sense of
presence with a minimal visual presentation of virtual
reality scenes and objects. The authors planned to use
physiometric indicators of sense of presence which are
readily quantifiable. The physiological instruments are
normally used to measure various changes in subjects'
bodily functions. The changes in bodily functions might
possibly be indicators of physiological arousal
purportedly linked to virtual reality sense of presence
and performance. For the purpose of monitoring the
subjects, researchers collected only the heart rate of
the subjects in this current experiment.

<u>Apparatus</u>

Hardware for this study consisted of a Pentium-
based™ computer (100 MHZ), Head-Mounted Display and
Head-Tracker (Virtual I/O™) so that the use could
interact with objects in the virtual world. Modeling was
done by using VREAM™ Virtual Reality Development
Software Package and Libraries (VRCreator™) to create
virtual reality scenes from the models which represented
a customized hierarchy of fear producing situations.

<u>Virtual Reality Scene</u>

Modeling was done by the VREAM™ Company under the
direction of the researchers. A model of auditorium
located in the CAU Research Science Building was created.

The virtual auditorium is 48 feet wide, 100 feet long and
55 feet high. The seating area has three sections of
chairs and can accommodate over 100 people. The software
was designed to allow the experimentor to bring the
audience into the auditorium one by one and then five at
a time until the auditorium was filled. Several audio
clips were programmed to respond to the speaker or create
a variety of situations for them to experience, such as
laughing, making comments, encouraging the speaker to
speak clearer or louder, ignoring the speaker and holding
conversations with others, and clapping hands at the end
or during the session. Specialized features created for
the facility included a virtual wooden podium with a
speaker's stand. An amplifier with direct connection to
the virtual reality software and hardware were used in
the therapy sessions. This enabled the subjects to hear
the echo of their voices. Simulations of the real echo in
the auditorium was created by a headphone attached to the
head-mounted display. The treatment schedule consisted of
five weekly sessions. The sessions lasted 10 to 20
minutes.

Treatment Procedure

        The treatment schedule consisted of five weekly
sessions for the VRT and comparison groups. The first two
sessions lasted 10 to 15 minutes and each of the three
subsequent sessions lasted 15 to 20 minutes. VRT
experiments were conducted in the Virtual Reality
Technology Laboratory on the CAU campus. Comparison group
experiments were partially conducted in the CAU
Psychology Department and Virtual Reality Technology
Laboratory. The comparison subjects reported for the
self-rated treatment expectancy and the repeated
assessment in the Psychology Department.
        In the first treatment session, the VRT subjects
were asked to rank order a list of public speaking

situations that induce fear, based on the degree of anxiety they arouse. These hierarchies were used later for the VRT (Pendleton and Higgins, 1983). During the VRT subjects' and comparison subjects' first session, they were individually familiarized with the virtual reality equipment and given several virtual reality demonstrations.

For the VRT subjects' subsequent sessions, individually therapy was conducted in a standard format. The computer program designed for VRT generated a standard hierarchy of fearful public speaking situations to be presented to the VRT group. Assessment measures were administered under blind conditions and in a standard order.

To assess the subjects, each of the two subjects groups were administered the ATPS and the modified SUD as pre-treatment, and post-treatment.

Subject Risk

The subject risk in this project was minimal. While there are some potential risks associated with virtual environment technology, as pointed out by Stanny (1995), definite steps were taken in this project to minimize these risks. According to Stanny, subjects at risk for psychological harm are primarily those who suffer from panic attacks, those with serious medical problems such as heart disease or epilepsy, and those who are or have recently been taking drugs with major physiological or psychological effects. As is previously stated, questions regarding these situations were asked as a part of the screening process, and persons with these characteristics were excluded from serving as subjects in this project. The project researchers are also aware that some people experience symptoms ranging from headache to epileptic seizure when exposed to visual stimuli which flicker at 8-12 Hz. This project did not use any frame update rates in this range. Furthermore, subjects were closely observed by experimenters at all times. If there had been any evidence of significant physical or psychological distress, the subject and the experimenter had the ability to quickly terminate the virtual environment session. Given these safeguards, and the fact that no subjects have experienced harm in the previous virtual environment studies at CAU, the researchers feel confident in saying that patient risk in this study was minimal and acceptable.

Consent

Written informed consent was obtained (1) prior to initial behavioral testing and (2) prior to beginning of treatment after the experimental procedures had been fully explained. Signed consent forms for all subjects were kept on secured file.

Results

Means and standard deviations of ATPS and SUD Pre-treatment and Post-treatment scores of VRT and comparison group subjects were calculated. The results and analyses of the assessment of before (base line) and after treatment are presented in Table 1. The strong correspondence between scores on the two instruments provides a good validity check, since the tests measures subjective discomfort on a 11-point scale, with the SUD being simply a rating of general discomfort and the ATPS measures discomfort on six emotional dimensions.

Comparisons of relevant sets of group means were performed using t-tests. No significant differences were seen between the pre-test scores of the two groups on their instrument, which indicated that the two groups were well matched as to initial severity of discomfort. There were also no significant difference between the pre-test and post-test scores of the comparison group on either test. This demonstrated that the severity of symptoms did not spontaneously change over the course of the experiment. Significant differences were found between the pre-test and post-test scores of the VRT group on both instruments, and between the post-test scores of the two groups on both tests. These means and t-test results indicate that the post-test scores of the VRT group were significantly lower than the pre-test scores and the post-test scores of the comparison group. This implies a reduction in the fear of public speaking symptoms as a result of the VRT treatment.

An examination of the correlation and the corresponding probabilities indicates that there was a significant relationship at the .05 level between the heart rate recorded and measure of subject unit of disturbance (SUD) scale. A Pearson Product-Moment Correlation coefficient (r) was used to measure the strength of the relationship ($r = 0.414$, $p = 0.05$).

Although somewhat limited, the present results are definitely important. They attest to the sense of presence experienced by subjects in the virtual environment. The degree of anxiety and habituation observed would not have occurred if the subjects had not been immersed in the virtual environment. The high SUD scores obtained during early training sessions indicate that the anxiety levels of subjects were raised through exposure to the virtual environments. The steady reduction in SUD scores across the training sessions indicate habituation (reduction in anxiety responses) as a result of the VRT treatment. With further research, the researchers believe that VRT may prove to be a cost-and-time-effective alternative to the treatment of phobic disorders.

Conclusion

The symptoms experienced by the subjects during virtual reality therapy mirror those which most speakers experience during a speech to a town meeting or

presentation at a business conference. They include an
increase in hear rate, lump in the throat, dry mouth,
sweaty palms, loss of balance, weakness in the knees,
etc.

It is apparent that the increase of anxiety at the
beginning of each level and session and steady reduction
after the subject spent some time in the virtual scene,
attest to sense of virtual presence. This pattern also
appeared in research studies with other phobic situations
and subjects. The subject definitely became immersed in
the virtual scene to the extend that they had to grasp a
hand rail in the laboratory to avoid falling and to
maintain their balance while they were in the virtual
environment. (North, North and Coble, 1995a; 1995b;
1996).

It is also not unusual for longer exposure to
virtual reality scenes to cause simulator sickness. This
is caused by discrepancies between visual and kinetic
perceptions; it is similar to motion sickness (Pausch et
al., 1992). Extended exposure to virtual reality may also
cause physical and psychological injury. With these
circumstances in mind, therapy sessions were limited to
10-20 minutes. This schedule was adopted to avoid any
physical and emotional discomfort the subject might
incur.

This study of the fear of public speaking
indicates that VRT is very effective in reducing self-
reported anxiety. The virtual reality therapy treatment
results in both a significant reduction of anxiety
symptoms (SUD and ATPS measurements) and the ability to
face the phobic situations in the real world. After the
treatment, subjects report that they have the ability to
speak comfortably in front of a crowd with greater
confidence.

This research project has the potential of
significantly increasing the range of the psychological
disorders that can be treated with VRT and, in turn,
enhancing the significant of the findings.

Discussion

Although the results of the above-mentioned research are very impressive, additional research in needed to conduct a more thorough investigation of this approach with other psychological disorders (e.g., PTSD, ADD, etc.). There is also a need to conduct extensive investigation of virtual reality in the treatment of psychological disorders by using methods that allow both objective and subjective measurements of anxiety to insure the validity of this research. Furthermore, if the funding are sufficient and remain constant, the researchers hope to investigate the influence of subject variables (demographic and personality characteristics) on the effectiveness of VRT. They also hope to include an imaginal systematic desensitization (conventional therapy) group in addition to the comparison and control groups used in current or previous studies.

One possible criticism of the results of VRT studies at CAU and elsewhere is that the measures of anxiety involved have been primarily, and often exclusively, subjective. There is evidence to suggest that subjective measures of anxiety (more specifically, ratings on the Subjective Units of Disturbance scale) have a high correlation with objective measures of anxiety (Thyer et al, 1984). This evidence was specifically evaluated in this study, where simultaneous subjective and objective measures of anxiety were obtained.

The current plan is to expand the research to a wider population and to extend the test site at the Virtual Reality Technology Laboratory in Atlanta to the Speech Improvement Company offices in Boston. This will allow the first known application of VRT technology to be held in a non-laboratory controlled setting with measurement in the real world.

Acknowledgements

This research project was sponsored by a grant from Boeing Computer Services (Virtual Systems Department), partially supported by U.S. Army Center of Excellence in Information Science under contract number DAAL03-92-6-0377 and The Speech Improvement Company. The views contained in this document are those of the authors and should not be interpreted as representing the official policies of the U.S. Government, either expressed or implied.

References

Abelson, J. L. and Curtis, G. C. (1989). Cardiac and neuroendocrine responses to exposure therapy in height phobics: Desynchrony within the physiological response system. Behavior Research and Therapy, 27, pp. 561-565.

American Psychiatric Association: Diagnostic and Statistical Manual of Mental Disorders, 4th Edition. Washington, D.C., American Psychiatric Association (1994).

Barfield, W., and Weghorst, S. (1994). The sense of presence within virtual environments: A conceptual framework. In Human-Computer Interaction: Software and Hardware Interfaces. G. Salvendy and M. Smith (Eds). Elsevier Publisher, pp. 699-704.

Marks, I. M. And Mathews, A. M. (1979). Brief standard self-rating for phobic patients. Behavior Research and Therapy, 17, pp. 263-267.

North, M. M. and North, S. M. (1994). Virtual environment and psychological disorders. Electronic Journal of Virtual Culture, 2(4), pp. 37-42.

North, M. M., North, S. M., and Coble, J. R. (1995a). Effectiveness of virtual environment desensitization in the treatment of agoraphobia. International Journal of Virtual Reality, 1(2), pp. 25-34.

North, M. M., North, S. M. and Coble, J. R. (1995b). A virtual reality application in the treatment of psychological disorders. Journal of Medicine and Virtual Reality, 1(2), pp. 28-32.

North, M. M., North, S. M. and Coble, J. R. (1996a). Effectiveness of virtual reality environment desensitization in the treatment of psychological disorders. PRESENCE: Teleoperators and Virtual Environments, 5(3), pp. 345-352.

North, M. M., North, S. M. and Coble, J. R. (1996b). Virtual Reality Therapy: An innovative paradigm. IPI Press: Colorado Springs.

Rothbaum, B. O., Hodges, L. F., Kooper, R., Opdyke, D., Williford, J. S., and North, M. M. (1995). Effectiveness of virtual reality graded exposure in the treatment of acrophobia. American Journal of Psychiatry, 152(4), pp. 626-628.

Thyer, B. A., Papsdorf, J. D., Davis, R., and Vallecorsa, S. (1984). Autonomic correlates of the subjective anxiety scale. Journal of Behavior Therapy and Experimental Psychiatry, 15, pp. 13-17.

Williford, J. S., Hodges, L. F., North, M. M. & North, S. M. (1993). Relative effectiveness of virtual environment desensitization and imaginal desensitization in the treatment of acrophobia. Proceedings of Graphics Interface '93 Conference, p. 162.

Wolpe, J. (1969). The Practice of Behavior Therapy. Pergamon Press: New York.

TABLE 1. Means (and Standard Deviations) and comparison of mean of Pre-test and Post-test Scores of Experimental and Control Group Subjects on the Public Speaking Questionnaire (Anxiety and Avoidance) and Attitudes Towards Public Speaking Questionnaire.

Measure [a]	Experimental Group (Received VRT Treatment)						Control Group (Did Not Receive VRT Treatment)					
	Baseline (N=6)		After 5 Weeks (N=6)		Analysis (df=10)		Baseline (N=8)		After 5 Weeks (N=8)		Analysis (df=14)	
	Mean	SD	Mean	SD	t	P	Mean	SD	Mean	SD	t	P
Public Speaking Questionnaire												
SUD scale												
Anxiety	6.17	2.32	1.17	0.75	5.03	<0.01	6.13	1.55	6.00	1.85	0.15	<0.02
Avoidance	5.00	1.67	1.50	1.23	4.13	<0.02	4.75	2.25	4.88	2.17	-0.11	<0.01
Attitudes Towards Public Speaking Questionnaire												
Bad	6.50	1.76	2.17	1.60	4.46	<0.01	5.75	2.12	6.13	1.55	-0.40	<0.03
Awful	6.67	2.07	1.83	1.60	4.53	<0.01	6.25	1.39	6.12	1.81	0.16	<0.04
Unpleasant	7.00	2.53	2.00	2.10	3.73	<0.01	6.63	1.77	7.0	1.85	-0.41	<0.03
Dangerous	6.00	2.37	1.33	1.75	3.88	<0.02	6.75	1.98	6.0	1.77	0.80	<0.02
Threat	5.67	2.73	1.50	1.23	3.41	<0.01	7.13	1.89	6.88	1.46	0.30	<0.03
Harmful	5.67	1.75	1.33	1.21	4.99	<0.01	5.88	1.81	6.38	1.51	-0.60	<0.02

[a] A higher rating indicates greater distress.

ABOUT THE AUTHORS
☙ ❧

Max M. North, Ph.D. is a tenured Associate Professor in the Computer Information Science Department and Director of the Human-Computer Interaction Group & Virtual Reality Technology Laboratory at Clark Atlanta University. He is the author of many articles in the field of computing and psychology and the recipient of an award from Sigma Xi, the Scientific Research Society. Dr. North's field of research is human-computer interaction. Specifically, his work focuses on studying "sense of presence" in virtual environments and designing virtual environments to study human-spatial perception and performance behavior in virtual environments. Dr. North's major contribution to the scientific community is his discovery and continuous strong research activities in the innovative area of virtual reality therapy which has received international attention and coverage in the scientific community and the popular media, including the *New York Times, U.S. News and World Report, PBS, NBC, ABC.*

Contact Information:
>   Max M. North, Ph.D.
>   Clark Atlanta University
>   Atlanta, GA 30314
>   Phone: 1-404-880-6942
>   FAX: 1-404-880-6963
>   E-mail: max@acm.org
>   URL: http://www.a2zsol.com/members/virtualreality

Richard A. Blade, Ph.D. is a professor of physics at the University of Colorado–Colorado Springs. Other professional positions include Caltech, University of California–Berkeley, and United States International University. Professor Blade serves as science editor for IPI Press and Editor-in-Chief of the International Journal of Virtual Reality. He also serves as Focus Chair for IEEE Standards in Virtual Reality and Chair of the Working Group on the Virtual Reality Glossary. His current research involves virtual reality motion simulation.

Contact information:
>   Richard A. Blade, Ph.D.
>   2608 N. Cascade Ave.
>   Colorado Springs, CO 80907
>   Phone: 719-471-4476
>   FAX: 719-630-1427
>   E-mail: rblade@mail.uccs.edu